Iron Horseman
level 1

by John Burke

Iron Horseman level 1 © copyright 2007 John Burke

First published in Great Britain in 2005 by
Black Belt Academy Ltd,
Newton Abbot, Devon, TQ12 2RX

Published by
Karate Academy Ltd
8 Signal Buildings, Brunel Road, Newton Abbot, Devon, TQ12 4PB, England

Printed and Bound in Great Britain

British Library Cataloguing in Publication
Data available

ISBN 095503406X

Warning:
Martial Arts can be dangerous. Practice should not be undertaken without first consulting your physician. Training should take place under the supervision of a qualified instructor. The contents of this book are for educational use and in no way do we endorse the use of the techniques herein. Practitioners need to be aware of the Law and how it pertains to "Use of Reasonable Force" in cases of self-defence. Remember, ignorance does not equate with innocence.

Dedicated
To those who support our journey.
Family, true friends,
Our teachers and our students.
Without them we couldn't be
Dedicated.

Other titles available

A Karate Primer
The Eikoku Karate-do Keikokai Grading Syllabus
Peaceful Mind
Fortress Storming

The Kata & Application DVD range
The syllabus DVD range

Interior photos by Steph Ellis
Thanks to Uke Richard Carrick sensei

Contents

Foreword by Patrick McCarthy Hanshi 7
Introduction 9

The Background 11
Tekki Shodan—the basis of application 17
The Common Methods of Attack 21

Section 1 29
Section 2 41
Section 3 55
Section 4 63
Section 5 69
Section 6 87
Section 7 99

Conclusions 105
Appendices 107

Foreword
by Patrick McCarthy Hanshi

Patrick McCarthy with the author in Torquay, 2007

It is the human body, its unique function and common anatomical weaknesses that provide the foundation upon which functional application practices were originally developed. It's really quite a simple formula and yet this truth remains a mystery to most karate enthusiasts. Understanding basic anatomical function allows any learner to recognize how the principles of common mechanics govern human movement---any and all empty-handed fighting can be reduced to percussive impact or seizing, and or combinations thereof. This knowledge also provides the basis for identifying anatomical weaknesses, another vital link in the chain of effective self-defence. The habitual acts of physical violence [HAPV] provide the reality-based contextual premise with which early pioneers developed prescribed fighting techniques to counter and control or submit an attacker. Tested and proven against varying degrees of aggressive resistance, effective fighting techniques and functional self-defence application practices were successfully forged from using the HAPV premise in two-person scenario drills.

A whole range of two-person application practices, to develop one's fighting and self-defence skills, were ultimately developed and placed into a system of learning. They included #1. Giving & receiving percussive impact [blunt force trauma], #2. Negotiating the clinch, #3. Joint manipulation, cavity seizing and limb entanglement, #4. Chokes and strangles [deprivation of air and blood], #5. Balance displacement, #6. Ground-fighting & submission, and #7. Escapes & counters.

Continued...

The idea of creating kata [solo re-enactments of the prescribed fighting and self-defence techniques] evolved from learners rehearsing these skills without a partner. By separating the two-person drills into identifiable attack scenarios [i.e. HAPV] and prescribed response sequences, pioneers successfully established solo re-enactment models. By linking together individual re-enactment models into collective routines pioneers developed unique and complex solo exercises through which to not only impart or culminate a lesson but also to express one's individual prowess while strengthening their overall mental, physical and holistic conditioning.

Based upon this mechanism, the work that lies before you delves into the application practices of the Tekki kata. Written by British karate researcher, Sensei John Burke, he is an instructor who has been successfully promoting his own findings in the United Kingdom. If you were impressed with the format of his other books, "Fortress Storming," and "Peaceful Mind," then I am confident you'll find this work a welcome addition to that information.

I'd like to congratulate Sensei John Burke on another fine contribution to our tradition. I hope that this new work finds it way out beyond the local Shotokan community and into the British karate community in general and ultimately beyond. Sensei Burke is man of integrity and a credit to our tradition and I am proud to be associated with teachers like him. As long as there is a need to better understand the application practices of kata there will always be a place for a work like this. I hope you'll enjoy this book as much as I have.

Patrick McCarthy
Hanshi 8th Dan
International Ryukyu Karate-jutsu Research Society
http://www.koryu-uchinadi.com
A link to the past is your bridge to the future
Life isn't about finding yourself -- it's about creating yourself. - GBS

Introduction

This book is about the study of Karate kata.

Now, Karate itself can be considered to be many things. Some see it as a sport, used for scoring points in combat or for demonstration. Some see it as a valid form of self protection. Some view Karate as a business, and others as an interesting hobby. Karate can be used as moving meditation, or an introspective way of looking at the world and one's own experiences.

It is no surprise, then to learn that the part of Karate known as kata also has a multitude of meanings, depending on whom you ask.

They are sets of moves connected together and performed by those practising martial arts. There have been so many misconceptions surrounding the practice of forms. Some see them as merely something that must be learned in order to pass their rank examination. Others view them as antiquated nonsense that has no place in a world where pads can be used instead. Some see kata as only suitable for demonstration and competitions—the prettier the form the more likely you are to win attention or a medal.

Some, like me, see kata as the storehouse of the old Karate masters' knowledge. The shorthand memory aid that grants you access to techniques which you cannot—must not—perform on a training partner with speed and power.

Kata = style

For kata to be necessary in these terms we can say that we are looking at them for self protection. If the moves were for sport then they could be practiced as sport with a partner without harm.

As we delve into these applications you will see that the attacker can move at full speed but that the defender has to look after their training partner's health, and as such cannot respond to the fullest.

By the end of the book I hope you will agree that kata are a vibrant and vital part of our art.

Kata = form

The kanji (Japanese writing) for the word kata depict

the idea of what kata is about. There are generally two ways to write kata. Our understanding is that the kanji illustrate a shape carved in the ground, or an idea that is passed down through time.

This gives us an idea that kata are like a mould that we pour ourselves into, shaping our movements into those prescribed as belonging to this form. There is room for individuality, but we must be careful of changing the tradition beyond recognition or much will be obscured.

We must understand that the kata developed as a way of recording movements/techniques when it was not advisable to write it down. They are shorthand representations of lessons learned from one's teacher—reminders of all we should know.

We're going to take a look at Tekki Shodan—Iron Horseman level 1. There has been plenty written about this form already. You can take my treatise on it as techniques that I have found to be useful in order to explain the kata. If you have heard that this kata was for fighting in an alleyway then we will question whether there isn't a more efficient way of fighting in an alleyway. If you have heard that it represents a samurai on horseback then I'm afraid that you have been misled. If you heard the one about it being based on the fighting system of the narrow walk-ways between paddy fields or the stance required for fighting on an Oriental junk then I'm glad you're still investigating other options.

We're going to take a look at options and variations of application. We base this on the idea that if Tekki Shodan was all that you knew, and your body was going to respond to aggression with moves that were ingrained, then the moves have to work against those attacks.

If you like our applications then Great! If you don't like them then I hope that the ideas presented here cause you to explore options in your training.

If we manage to inspire you to look deeper into your kata then we'll have done our job.

The Background

At the end of this book we'll mention some more about the background and origins to kata,
Generally, Karate is said to be Japanese. We know that it was taken to mainland Japan by the pioneers of modern Karate, primarily Funakoshi Gichin, the nominal founder of the Shotokan style.
Funakoshi was an Okinawan. He heralded from the island that is located about midway between Japan, China, and Taiwan. It can be said that culturally, Okinawa was a great melting pot, being dominated at various times in its history by both Japan and China, it was also one of the first Japanese places to have dealings with westerners.

Tekki Shodan is known as a Shotokan kata. Versions of it are also taught in Shitoryu, Wadoryu, and Shorinryu styles of Karate, and also in Taekwondo. There are huge similarities to some Kung Fu forms, too.

The older name for Tekki Shodan was Naihanchi ナイハンチ. Unfortunately, Naihanchi's earliest reference in written form has the word written in Hiragana. The Hiragana style of writing is phonetic—it tells you how to pronounce the word. This is unfortunate because if the name was written in Kanji there would be an idea conveyed alongside it. That idea might be the meaning of the kata or a feeling, but it would give us a little something more to go on.
Without proof then, no-one can say what Naihanchi actually means. There is a strong likelihood that it refers to "inside" with the *Nai* portion of the name. If the root is Chinese, as most Karate kata have their root in Chinese forms, then it could well be Nai Fuan Chuan—inside fighting. This then, gives us a strong clue to the nature of the kata. For the fighting to happen inside it does not necessarily mean indoors—although it is suited to enclosed environs. Inside is more likely a reference to the idea that you are already in someone's grip, or within range. Although I will show you some applications from the outside of an attacker's sphere of influence, they also work just as well when the attacker has us firmly grasped.

Patrick McCarthy sensei has discovered a reference to the use of the term **_Te_** prior to the name change to the modern version. We are already aware of the fact that **_Karate_** 空手 used to be known as **_Todi_** 唐手 .

And it seems natural for us to see the link between the China Hand and the Empty Hand evolution of the term. But when the art was just known as Ti, the definition as "hand" was only part of the translation. You see, ti can also be about _technique_, about _art_, about _ryu_—or tradition—and about _form_. This _ti_ is often turned into the honorific form **_nchi_** その敬語は ンチ

This is not so much a Japanese rendition as belonging to the dialect specifically found around _Shuri_ and _Naha_. These two centres of Okinawa have more or less merged in the current day, but were known as different places with different lineages of ti prior to the 1900s. Naha te was written 那覇手 with kanji, but we have no record of the kanji for Naihanchi.

While I am no historian nor a linguist, and the research can and certainly will go further, Tobey Reed sensei of the USA made the connection that **Naha nchi** might have been the old name for Tekki, thus relating to the _ti_ of _Naha_ town. Now, as we know that Miyagi of **_Goju Ryu_** (almost exclusively Naha-te) used to practice a version of Tekki we can see that there is a link.

The Tekki Shodan interpretation has a number of interesting features. The predominant use of kibadachi 騎馬立ち(horse-riding stance). Before being renamed Tekki Shodan, the kata was called Kibadachi kata for a while.

Sideways movement on a single line. Most kata have more complicated _embusen_ (performance lines). Moving to the right before moving to the left. Many kata move to the left before going to the right. Interestingly, this kata still has the performer move their left foot first, it's just a cross step instead of a direct step outwards.

There also exist Tekki Nidan and Tekki Sandan. Some say that Funakoshi's teacher, Itosu Anko created the second and third kata. There is also a theory that the original Naihanchi consisted of all the movements found in Tekki 1-3, and that it has just been split to aid learning.

Yabu Kentsu was a student of Itosu, and was known as "the Sergeant". He was known to have told his students 'Karate begins and ends with Naihanchi' and that they must practice the kata 10,000 times to make it their own. This shows how important the practice of the proto-Tekki was considered.

On the other hand, Nakayama Masatoshi, the former head of the renown JKA says in Best Karate "The Tekki kata are rather tedious, so turn your head briskly". This sells the kata short, doesn't it? Why keep it at all if it's so laborious that the best thing about it is how fast you turn your head?

Motobu Choki, student of Itosu and contemporary of Funakoshi, clearly states that Naihanchi is a "style" of Karate.

Funakoshi states that the kata can take a minute to perform, yet performance at club level tends to last between 15 and 20 seconds.

Funakoshi was said to have spent 9 years training in Naihanchi. You must believe that there was depth to his training or ask what he was up to for all that time.

As a kata that is associated with the rank of 4th kyu, Tekki Shodan is usually practiced for 3-6 months before the student moves on to the more flamboyant Bassai Dai. Is this appropriate? Should it be cast aside so quickly?

So from the JKA we have Tekki, and they claim to have received it from Funakoshi. He learned it from Itosu, who may have been taught it by Matumura Sokon. Matsumura may have learned it from a Chinese man living in the Okinawan town of Tomari, or maybe not. Matsumura was the bodyguard to three successive

Okinawan kings. Itosu also worked in the Royal court. One wing of the palace was dedicated to visiting Chinese dignitaries, a building behind the palace was set aside for Japanese dignitaries. Martial practice occurred on the parade ground/forecourt in front of the building. Matsumura or Itosu could equally have learned any of their martial skills from Chinese or Japanese bodyguards or soldiery.

Matsumura's teacher was "Todi" Sakugawa, Todi being a nickname equivalent to Karate. China Hand Sakugawa is the source for a number of kata.

The kata appears to feature a number of hand positions shown in Kung Fu (or, more appropriately, Chuan Fa). The horse-riding stance is also used hugely in some style of kung fu, including Hung Gar.

Through his research into Bagua Zhang, an "internal" style of Chinese martial art, my good friend and my senior in martial arts—Neil Ellison sensei—has shown me huge parallels between Bagua and Tekki Shodan. Particularly the Eight Mother Palms form. Neil is one of the martial arts' biggest secrets, able knowledgeable, and modest. He and Stuart Howe sensei teach their remarkable blend in Teesside, in the UK.

In all likelihood, then, Tekki originates in the Chinese martial arts, and through there we may draw tenuous links back to the Shaolin temple and Bodhiharma, the Indian monk who is alleged to have taught the monks their legendary fighting skills. Of course, as a member of Indian royalty, he must have been exposed to Vajramushti, and perhaps Kalaripayattu. Perhaps the origins are there.

Or when Alexander the Great invaded India, did he bring fighting skills with him? Or the pictures on the inside of the Great Pyramid at Giza—the ones that look like people doing Tekki while they are fighting—did they influence the Geek civilization, the Romans, and all who came after?

Perhaps we are better off admitting that people have been fighting since before they were really people, and that the tools we have on our body are our principle weapons, alongside anything we can get hold of. The Okinawans knew how to fight before the Chinese arrived there, the Chinese knew before Bodhidharma was even born. Yes there may be great influences from people and peoples at work, and certain positions and shapes occur universally, but development of a style—or a kata - does not occur in a linear fashion, but rather is shaped by every influence that happens to it.

the Basis of Application

Tekki Shodan

The Basis of Application

The movements of your kata each have meaning. They were originally put together to remind students of self-defence acts that they had practised before their teacher. There may be many applications for any one movement, and on our seminars we might teach slightly more advanced versions depending on which students are present.

Let's consider what we must know before we look at the applications that the kata gives us:

As we are not considering applications that are only based around sport we will not be looking at the rule-bound arena.

This means that we will not consider the kind of attack that another martial artist would make. Very rarely would anyone who is a trained martial artist attack another person without good cause. The kind of attacker who thinks they are a martial artist is unlikely to be effective if they are the kind of person who attacks people like us. Hence, roundhouse kicks to the head and reverse punches in a nice low front stance will not be responded to with moves from this kata.

Instead, we have to look at the real distance and kind of attack that we will need to defend against.

Our response must be instant, for if the fight becomes prolonged there is more risk of injury to ourselves. This means that we will discard anything which leaves the attacker able to effectively continue to fight after the initial moment of contact.

For each movement to represent a self defence situation we will see that the types of situation reflect commonly occurring attacks.

Common themes in our applications include:

- Beginning at a range where there is a real danger of being struck by any of the attacker's weapons.
- Only using common methods of attack which an untrained attacker might reasonably be expected to use.
- Beginning at a casual guarded position rather than "in a stance".
- Making both hands work together—never leaving one hand "ready" or "pulling back to make the other hand more powerful".
- Making contact with the attacker half-way through the technique—not at the end.
- Penetration with each technique, not just surface contact.
- Leaving no gap between the attacker and our own body when seeking to control them.

Co-ordination of Mind, Breath, and Body.

When analysing the pattern of attacks which occur "in the street" we see that there will usually be a pre-amble/"interview"/set-up/distraction which is verbal. The trained martial artist must recognise these factors and use it to raise his energy level from casual to "primed for action". This does not mean jump in to a full zenkutsu-dachi. Being ready is a state of mind—preparedness. I recommend that you look at the works of Geoff Thompson (particularly the *Fear* book) for a full analysis of the anatomy of a confrontation.

We must attend to the common types of attack that Patrick McCarthy (8th Dan) hanshi refers to as the Habitual Acts of Physical Violence. These are the types of attack that occur time and time again and are initiated by those who use aggression against unsuspecting innocents.

- Hook **punches**, straight punches, upper-cuts
- Single wrist **grab**, cross-body wrist grab, double wrist grab
- Grab at the forearm, elbow, or shoulder; either one-handed or two-handed
- **Pushing**, single-handed or two-handed from the front, side, or rear.
- Bear-hug grabs from the front, side, or rear; over the arms or under them.
- Strangulations/neck-grabs; one-handed, two-handed, from the front, side, or rear
- Grabbing the groin.
- Head-**locks**; facing forwards or backwards
- Full-Nelson or half-Nelson locks from the rear, or Rugby tackle rushes from the front or side.
- Head-butt.
- Back-handed strikes, slaps
- Descending strikes or slaps
- **Kicks** to the shin or thigh
- Knee to the groin

The many variations on the above which may come from types of clothing or situation might also be investigated, but recognise the core principle: an assault is when one of the above methods enters within your personal space.

Recognise the attack's imminence and prepare to react to it. Know the effects of adrenaline and how they manifest. Have your plan ready and be prepared to see it through. As explained in the previous section; strikes from behind can only be deflected if you are psychic or there is some kind of warning (shadow/reflection/ verbal abuse, etc.). If you manage to turn then it is no longer an attack from the rear.

Hopefully, all martial artists understand that where an application is shown with the right hand it could be performed equally with the left. There is a remarkable near-symmetry to this kata, which means that the applications will be shown for one side of the kata. That means that you reverse the hand positions to show the other part of the kata.

The ground rules:

- **If you can avoid the confrontation, do.**

- **If you can talk your way out of it before it gets messy, do.**

- **If you can hit, pre-emptively or otherwise, then escape, do.**

- **If you hit an attacker and it doesn't finish it then use the time you buy yourself to use your technique. An aggressor will be more compliant if you have already hit him.**

- **If one technique does not fulfill your requirements use another. Don't stop. Carry on until you are safe. Kata applications show a snap shot of action, not the whole fight.**

- **If you can, move to a position of relative safety/strength (off-line rather than directly in front of his "other" fist).**

- **Safety first. Practice the moves with speed, power, and visualisation only on a bag or thin air, not on a partner. This is what kata are for. When practicing on empty air don't lock out joints, use your muscles to stop the movement. When practising with a partner, start slowly and gently, and only increase the speed and intention with experience and to your partner's comfort threshold.**

Common Methods of Assault

Here you can see the kind of distance that the confrontation begins at, and you can understand that our hands are raised. While the aggressor gesticulates and threatens, the defender tries to calm the situation and makes sure that there is a reaction distance between the two.

This distance is usually no more than one arm's length when the threat becomes real. Any further than that and we are still at talking distance; any closer and we will have begun to scuffle already.

Often there will also be a sensing and provoking hand, both to invade your space and to Intimidate you. This is a precursor to the actual bodily harm, but common assault has already taken place.

Grabs come in all shapes and sizes.

The grab is usually designed to pull you onto a further attack, but could also be harmful in itself if it is a choke or strangle.

Often our advice is to keep any hands that touch you pinned against you where they land, but you must understand that being able to continue to Breath, and continue to have Circulation of Blood is more important than retaining the attacker's limb.

With more honest grabs it is always the other limbs that are more threatening than the one which landed on you.

Of course, grabs can occur in all sorts of places—both wrists; across the body or the same side of the body; on the upper arm (the number one most common grab used against women); and of course the restraint from the rear commonly called the bear hug!

These situations occur when we try to walk away from the danger and the attacker won't allow it. They are a prime signal that the situation is rapidly escalating and that physical harm is imminent. Any of them, even the bear hug, could be innocent—an attempt to stop you from doing something foolish, perhaps, but with a little bit of awareness we should be able to tell the difference between aggression and protection.

Of course, some grabs give you a better indication than others that there is violence afoot!

The lunging rugby-tackle type of attack is rarely mistaken for a cuddle.

Grabbing hair from the front or the rear can easily be exchanged for grabbing an ear if you don't have any hair. The Japanese book the Bubishi (as translated by Patrick McCarthy) also refers to a beard grab. Keep that one in mind, if it's relevant, as another alternative that you might have to defend against.

By here we can say that our awareness has failed us and the fight is on.

 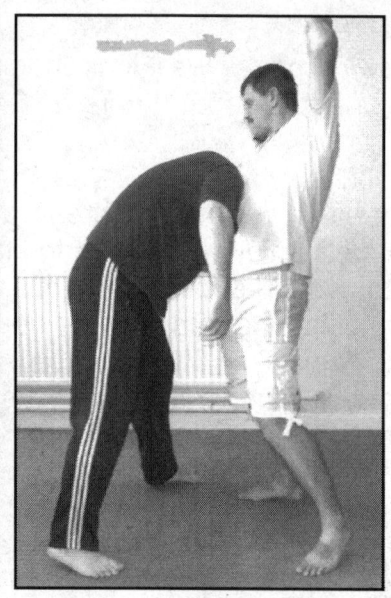

Grappling is also a form of grabbing, and occurs during the fight, usually, rather than as an initial entry into the situation. Someone could just come up and grab you into a headlock, but it is more likely to occur while you are moving around and the scrap has begun. The range changes dramatically and before you know it you can smell them.

Sometimes the threatening hand can gesticulate but not touch you. This might lead straight into the swinging hook punch. This won't be a boxer's punch or a martial artist's punch, but is more likely to be the wild un-controlled haymaker of yore. That's a blessing for us, because it is easier to detect the approach of an untrained punch as long as we are aware of the attacker at all.

On the following pages we'll look at various situations with regard to the kind of attacks that the Tekki Shodan kata can be used to counter.

Included in each description are Traditional Chinese Medicine details of targets. You don't have to know about the chi/ki system to be able to use the applications. It's entirely possible to achieve great results using modern western nomenclature for the targets.

Those of us who study the use of Pressure Points, however, train to deliver the retaliations to specific spots that conform to the laws of the body as it was understood at the time and place of the birth of these martial arts. As a method of visualising the effects and the techniques we find that TCM is a great aid.

Please don't think of it as anything mystical or religious, it's simply another way of naming and recognising what happens under the attack circumstances.

As Modern Western Medicine finds its way in the world, we see that it more closely matches the view that the Oriental systems came up with centuries ago. Nowadays we hear that your diet must conform to your blood type and your mental state is reflected in your physical state, etc.

The terminology that we will use has the body covered with **meridians**.

Each of these *energy channels* has an affinity with a particular **organ** or **bowel** of the body.

Each organ or bowel is aligned with either *positive* or *negative*, male or female, types of energy. These opposites are termed **yang** and **yin** and they are usually represented by that well known symbol which is actually called *taichi*– great universal.

The meridians are also labelled with their affinity to a certain type of energy, regarded as having properties matching the following *Elements*—**Fire, Earth, Water, Wood**, and **Metal**. That doesn't mean that those elements are actually in your body, but that the energy has characteristics that identify it in this way,

You can see the correlation below: yin meridians are in *italics* and yang meridians are **bold**.

Fire—*Heart, Pericardium*, **Small Intestine**, and **Triple Warmer**
Earth—*Spleen*, and **Stomach**
Metal—*Lung*, and **Large Intestine**
Water—*Kidney*, and **Bladder**
Wood—*Liver,* and **Gallbladder**

The list above, Fire-Earth-Metal-Water-Wood, represents the natural order of things as it is perceived by the TCM system. This is the *cycle of creation.*

The damaging way of using these meridians is called the *Cycle of Destruction,* and runs as follows: Fire-Metal-Wood-Earth-Water.

Some people say that you cannot hit such precise targets in a fight. We would say that this is precisely what you train for—the repetition of technique to target builds the code into your muscles to make it happen. If you only train to hit a face then it could be anywhere. Train to hit Stomach 4 and you are more likely to get that target with it's relevant effects.

The map of these pressure points are available in most acupuncture books. If they are not relevant to you then you don't need them, and if they are relevant to you then you will seek them out.

Section 1
Performance:

In performance of the kata, we use the yoi position and salutation to bring together our thoughts and our body into a disciplined mode.

This is the time to ensure that posture is correct; that heels, knees, and hips, spine, and head are in alignment.

The body should be neither locked nor too lax, possessing the ability to begin to move, as the term "ready" would suggest.

From the "shizentai" position, bring your feet together and bow, demonstrating respect for any examiner, for the kata, and for the effort that you are about to demonstrate.

Name the kata "Tekki Shodan" in a proud voice, displaying the spirit that you intend the performance to convey.

Calmly bring your hands across your body to meet in front of your belt knot. They should be away from your body, your arms at approximately 45 degrees. Your arms must not be locked straight or you will hamper your breathing.

The left hand goes on top of the right , the middle finger of each hand has the nail aligned with the other. The rest of the fingers lie closed but are allowed a natural angle.

The feet remain together, the tail-bone is tucked in and the knees are allowed to relax slightly.

Section 1

Yoi

Yoi means "ready" in Japanese, and is the command given for you to assume the posture shown here.

The so-called ready position for this kata is not the kind of position you would want to stand in if someone were being aggressive in front of you. It is not ready to do any defensive move.

While there is a place for claiming that the posture is designed to show the mental preparation that you go through, we choose to present responses to violence that duplicate the posture and feeling of Tekki Shodan's yoi position.

Version one

So, we take our response to an attack—the kata move—and see what it can do.

Oyo Principle: the attacker is at a distance where they are able to hit you.

Oyo Principle: we do not begin by standing in any stance but the natural one, with one foot slightly in front of the other.

This is not how the kata begins, this is prior to the kata beginning.

At his stage we come to realise that there will be ensuing violence. In order to protect ourselves, or perhaps our loved ones, we decide that the following action is necessary and justified.

Oyo Principle: go through what is or is not justified in your mind a long time before any conflict actually comes. There isn't much time for decision making when in front of an attacker.

The attacker reaches towards us.

Subconsciously he wishes to test our defensive capabilities. He doesn't know it, but what he is doing is, on a primal level, destabilising our equilibrium.

Being aware of his actions—more than he is—we can short-circuit the process that is hard wired into him to generate aggression.

Meeting the attacker's approaching left hand—his testing hand—with our left hand, we immediately bridge his wrist with our other hand.

Our left hand pushes down, and initially towards ourselves while our right hand keeps the attacker's left elbow aimed inwards across their body, thus preventing them from turning fully with their attacking right hand.

effort

Our hands are the pivot and the effort. The load is the attacker's body, the lever is his arm.

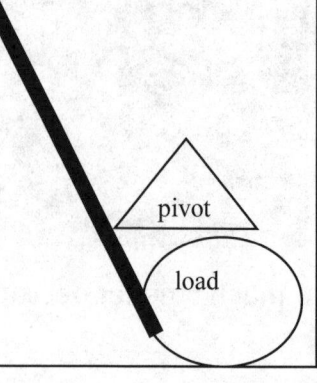

pivot

load

This shows exactly why the arms must angle inwards as they do in the performance.

Oyo Principle: the further from the base of the joint pressure is exerted, the less strength is needed. It's leverage.

Oyo Principle: cross body motor reaction stops the other hand from being used immediately.
We drive the attacker to the floor.

Oyo principle; the smaller the circle, the nastier the lock.

Oyo Principle: work through the quadrants of the body when seeking a direction to move the attacker in.

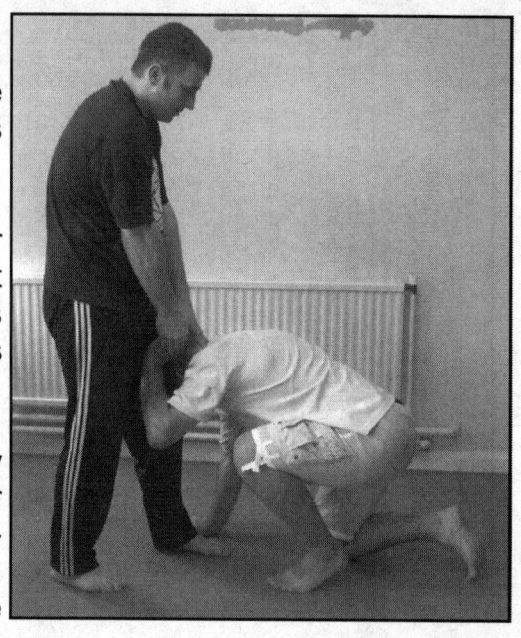

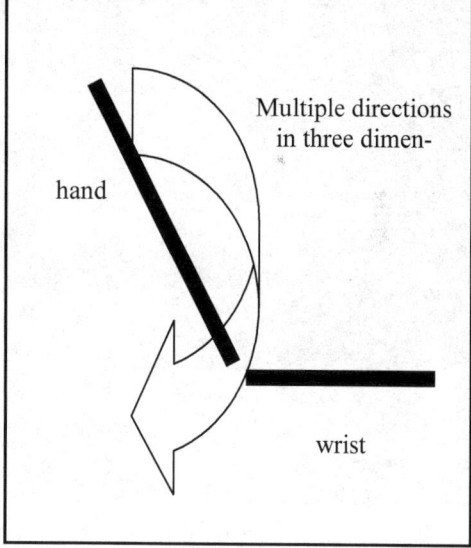

hand

Multiple directions in three dimen-

wrist

TCM: Fire and metal, the wrist points and LI3

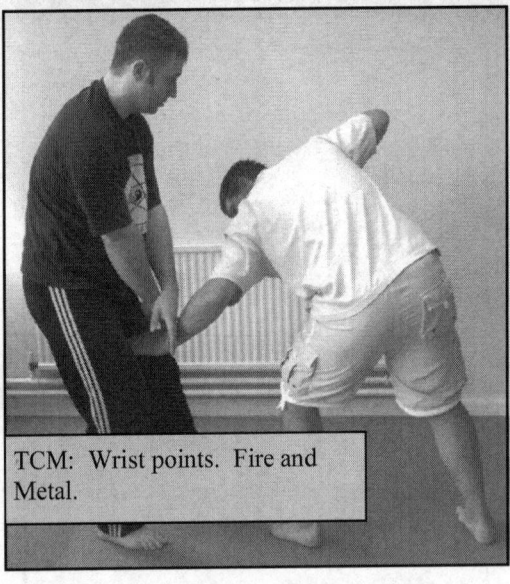

TCM: Wrist points. Fire and Metal.

Version two

The attacker has already made contact with their probing hand. In doing this we are given a point of contact and a method of manipulation of the opponent.

We initially clasp it to us and begin to turn our body to the outside line while pressing down.

Oyo Principle: when we move backwards as a flinch reaction we don't just go with our natural reaction, but channel the action into something useful.

Oyo Principle: If possible, seek the outside line, seek the "blindside". This moves us away from any other weapon.

Oyo Principle: The balance is affected by multi-directional effort.

Version 3

In this scenario, the testing hand is neglected by the attacker.

Without further ado, the attacker tries to land their classic right hook through our jaw.

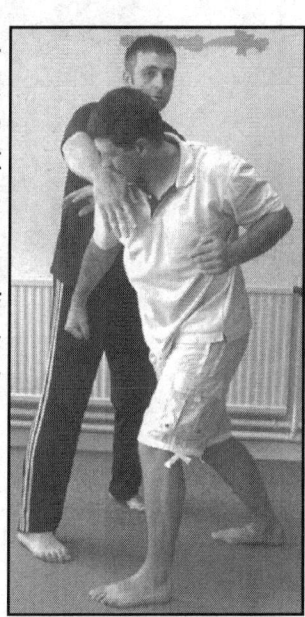

Using the flinch re-action to gain us a moment, we place the soft block without offering strength as resistance.

On this occasion we allow the attacker's arm to pass over the top of the guard to place us on their outside line; our block folds, directing the attacker's effort over our head.

This is also used to press their arm down— here, we're still looking at the position prior to the beginning of the kata.

Having brought the attacker past us, we slip in behind him.

Our hands go to both sides of the attacker's neck. The number of ways this can be used as a strike is truly frightening.

- We can bring the hands together and allow the forearms to attack the sternoceido mastoid.
- We can allow the ridge-hand to attack the carotid sinus,
- We can use the palms to shock downwards onto the sternum.

Care must be taken in practice, as with all techniques, but especially when working above the heart.

Any of these can be used to fully incapacitate the opponent, especially if stepping backwards at the same time.

TCM: PC6?LI10 or 11
CV18-22, S9, LI18
Fire, Metal, Earth.

TCM: CV4-7

Version 4

As the attacker has grabbed at our clothing—perhaps the lapels if we are wearing a jacket—we take our hands and bring them together to reinforce the fingers as a striking area.

As our hands pass under the attackers' arms he is less able to detect our intent; he can't see clearly.

This is important because the groin area is protected by a strong reflex action that we will circumvent by striking while the attacker can't see.

Our fingers are guided by clothing, especially if the opponent is wearing a large metal belt buckle, towards the area of the bladder. Our aim is to project in and down—45 degrees is a good angle—in order to affect the bladder.

Warning—do not practice this move on women. There is a huge possibility that you will affect the womb. No-one deserves that.
There is a slight danger that the opponent will bring their head violently forward as you do this move. By bringing you own face well back there is less chance of being head-butted. By twisting slightly you may even be able to use your shoulder to receive the head for extra impact.

 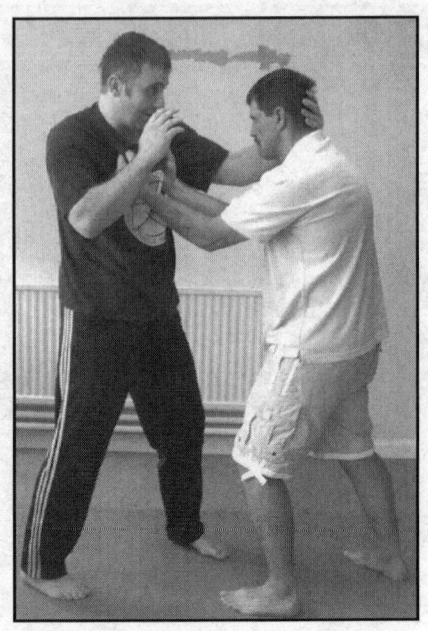

Version 5

Without the arm length to immediately attack the bladder, we rely upon taking the attacker's intention more directly.

Striking down on the head is a form of BAR that we often employ, but in this case it fits right into the kata, particularly if you are aware of the more Okinawan style of producing the first posture. You bring the hands up and fold them down.

Even as the opponent jostles for position, we ensnare their head. With two hands in contact we can move backwards—stealing balance - and pull their head down.

Continued...

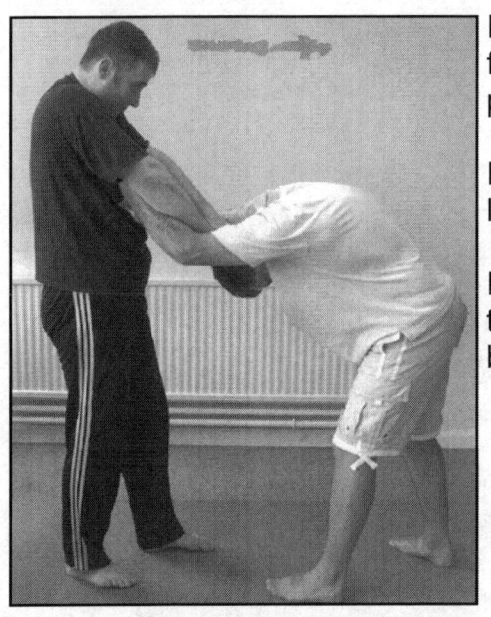

If at all possible, we need to force the head down and then push it away.

In this way we treat the spine like a concertina.

It is important to realise that this is not a matter of strength, but of technique.

TCM: GB20, GV

Section 2
Performance

The kata progresses with an abrupt crossing of the ankles. The left foot steps across to the right. We have found it very helpful to concentrate on the compression feeling and the use of the inner thigh rather than on the position and movement of the foot.

The weight is not placed onto the left foot until we are *ready*. We certainly do not just step over without control.

Raising the right knee directly in front of the body, *hizageri*, our arms cross, the right hand underneath.

The right hand swings out while the left makes *hikite* -returning hand— and the foot stamps down, *fumakomi*. Even though the movement is a stamp, our self control should allow us to place the foot on the floor.

Swing the top half of the body to the right, making sure that the knees move no more than one inch, slamming the left elbow into the waiting right hand. *Mawashi empi uchi*.

Looking abruptly to the left, bring the hands to the "cup-and-saucer" position, *koshi gamae*.

The left hand goes directly from the hip, outwards and downwards to the left. An abbreviated *gedan barai*.

It is swiftly followed by a sharp, short punch, *kagezuki*. The right wrist is no further left than the outside line of the body.

These last two moves follow each other very quickly.

Section 2

Side step, knee lift, stamp, back-hand, elbow, hip guard.

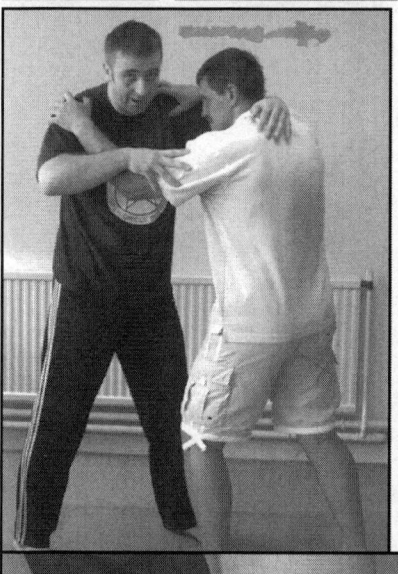
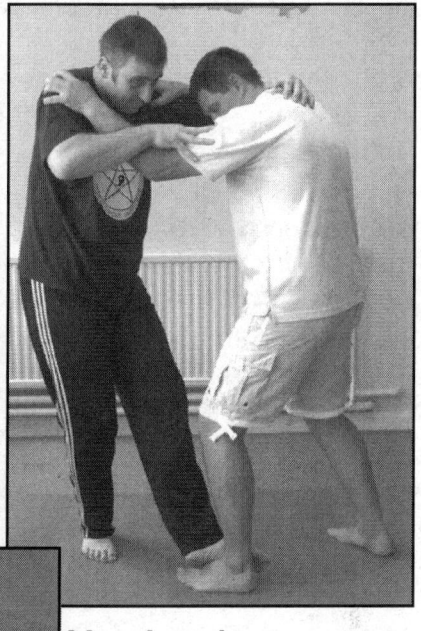

Version 1

Looking at this kata as a series of "close in" techniques affords us the right to call it a grappling kata. It can, of course, be used for other things, too.

As the grapple continues, we get smart enough to use a multi-layered approach.

Attacking on one plane can usually be resisted, attacking multiple heights on multiple planes usually cannot.

Controlling their balance, we swiftly deliver our front foot across the ankle.

Even if we do not smash the opponent's ankle with our inside-sweep, we should still cause enough of a distraction so that our knee attack is not countered.
The targets for the knee are variable—groin, thigh, abdomen—even the head if it is low enough.

As the knee descends, the foot should make further contact with the opponent. It could be as little as raking the inside of their calf or shin with the sole of our foot, or as bad as smashing straight through the knee.

If the knee is missed, then the foot should still catch the inside of the ankle, but even if it only stomps on their foot, we will have served a purpose.

Oyo principle: redundancy. Even if the technique doesn't go to the exact location we want, it will still serve.

TCM: SP6, GB/LV crossing.
Earth and wood.

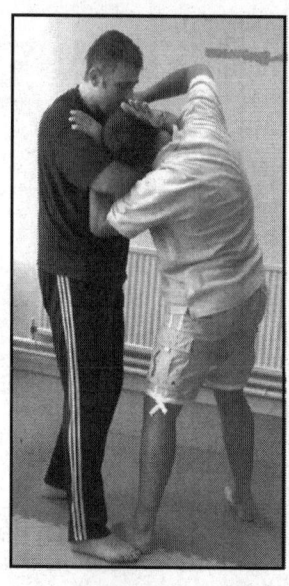  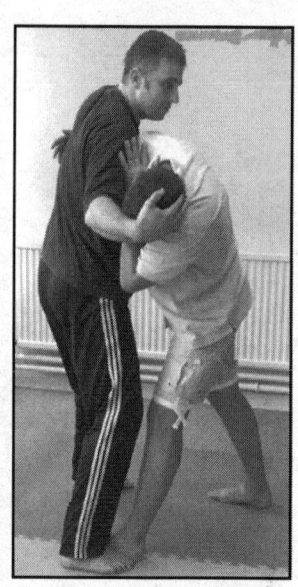

Before the side-step is completed, the hands may have been able to do some work.

We bring both hands across the head, sure to slap front and back.

Again we are disorienting the opponent before they can do anything else—another form of BAR.

Our right arm swings out, using the back of the forearm to smash or the ulna side to cut into the opponent.

Grabbing their head, we bring our elbow smashing into it.

We guide by touch, so that in the confusion we do not need to see the attacker's head, we merely bring our own limbs together.

TCM: GB20 & GB cluster. B10 & B1. Wood and Water.

Following on from the elbow strike to the head, we maintain that contact and wrench the head down towards our hip.

Bringing the head of the attacker down to one side is all about changing their balance. With their hips no longer directly beneath their head we know that their balance is severely reduced.

The head is taken through multiple angles and planes to accomplish this.

The move that appears to be a short downward block can then be used to completely unbalance the attacker and pull them across, lining them up for a short, sharp punch in the throat.

TCM: GB cluster, S9/LI18
Wood, Earth, Metal

Version 2

In this scenario the attacker has grabbed our wrists with our hands in an upward position. This can occur as a response to our attack to their eyes or face, or as they try to force their potential victim up against a wall, for instance.

We trap their hand against our wrist. Doing this involves reaching across our body, and because we are bending our elbows, the attacker cannot prevent the action. As their own hand crosses their centre-line involuntarily, the attacker finds that head-butting and kneeing becomes more difficult.

Oyo Principle: the opponent crossing the centreline involuntarily confuses them momentarily. It's why we don't cross our hands on the steering wheel.

We then bring our elbow into contact with their elbow. This is a prime example of how we can make the technique as controlling or damaging as we need to. How hard should be the elbow contact?

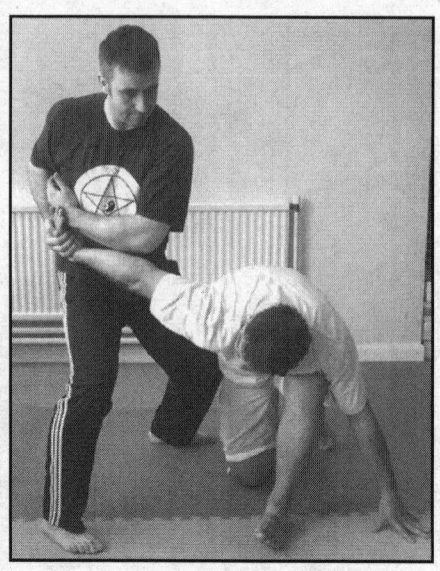

We following the attacker's arm to his fingers, dragging our forearm along his. The downward pressure and hyper-extension of his elbow causes the attacker to drop. As the grip is cross-body, so too does the attacker's other arm move away, preventing further attack.

This movement produces a burning sensation that lends itself nicely to the TCM idea of "adding fire".

We can manipulate his wrist to effect a wrist lock. This is achieved by turning the attacker's palm upwards and directing his fingers towards his upturned elbow.

In the example shown, our right hand holds the attacker's right wrist. The grip is from the outside of the wrist.

Following his arm back towards the attacker's head, we strike with the short gedan barai type of movement. This type of strike does not rely on sight, but rather on touch/feeling.

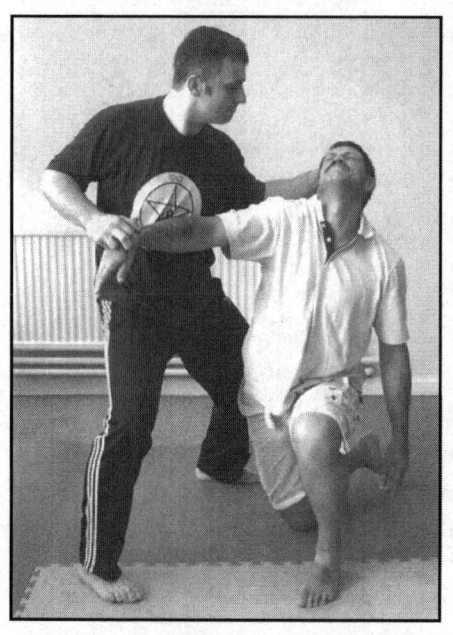

Oyo Principle: Having made contact, we maintain contact.

The advantage of this is to extend the attacker's tendons with the contact from our arm and our body, weakening his position

The strike here is directed towards the jaw, but also bears the back of the head, depending on how the opponent falls.

Arranging the target via his hair or ear we can then resort to the punch.

Targets for the punch might include the jaw or eye, but more effectively we can use the throat as our target.

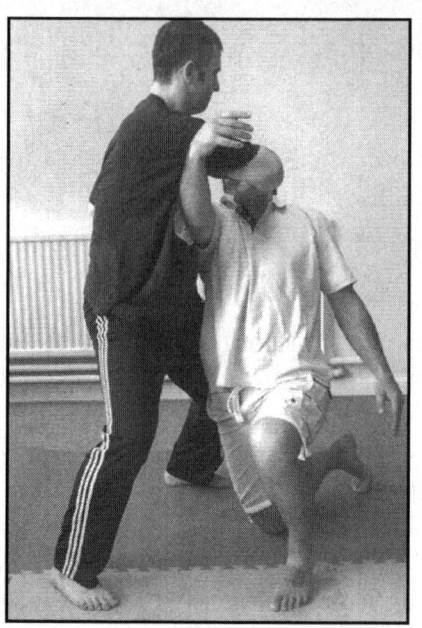

TCM: Wrist points, TW11, LI3,S6, S9 GB20 Fire, Metal, Earth., Wood

Version 3

In this situation we are dealing with someone who knows a little about punching. They try a right cross.

This action can also be seen to represent any straight line use of the arm. A jab might move at a different speed, but it follows the same path as the cross. The same can be said of the push and many grabs (especially to the lapel).

In training we can use the same retaliation against any straight-line attack, which allows us more adaptability and ingrains the technique rather than the situation.

We slip to the side fractionally and parry off with our outside hand.

Allowing us options, the hand nearest to the attacker is still free and available for initial strikes and/or distraction moves. These may not be covered by the kata as they are taken to be common sense for all martial artists. The kata only needs to cover the moves which need to be trained.

Maintaining that initial contact, we guide the hand down towards our opposite hip and ensnare it with the other hand.

Ideally, we latch at the wrist, ensuring that we seize nerves against bone, causing the wrist to relax and the fist to release.

As this is happening, we can see how the attacker is redirected so that any further attack would have to cross his own arm, and how with very little movement on our part we are effectively on the blind side of the aggressor.

Setting that wrist at our hip, we have stolen the opponent's balance.
By bringing our elbow into contact with their elbow we can also apply pressure to the elbow.

By varying degrees, we can press down on them, or drop the elbow more violently to actually cause damage to their arm.

Anyone who relies on this position for too long may find that the attacker wrestles free and manages to stand. By varying the use of the elbow and the tightness of the wrist–lock we can cause the attacker to experience every level of pain as if it was for the first time. Off and on, like a light-switch. You eyes can get used to bright light. They can get used to darkness. It is the rapid change from one to another that causes us to blink and squint.

We need to do this with his lock, so that he cannot become accustomed to the degree of pain as it is always changing.

Version 4

The attacker has placed their hand on us, grabbing at clothing, ready to punch us.

There are many distraction techniques that we could and should use, most of which will cause the grabbing hand to lose it's effectiveness.

In this case I passed my fingers very close to Richard's eyes.

Reaching over the top of his arm, we seize the wrist and turn it over. Not only is this done with the arm, but the hips come into play too. We also don't pull the hand too much away from us, but by the most direct route back to our hip. This can have the effect of locking the attacker's wrist momentarily against our chest as we make the change from his palm to the back of his hand against us.

The so-called hook punch that is performed next is used to directly strike or press against the opponent's elbow. The punch is characterised by it's downward angle (here hugely exaggerated) that tells the attacker exactly which direction we want them to move in.

We need to be aware that many moves in kata have, over time, had their hand shapes changed. The usual one is that open hands have become fists. In many cases this has occurred to keep the kata formal and neat, and to prevent students from breaking their hands when hitting pads or makiwara.

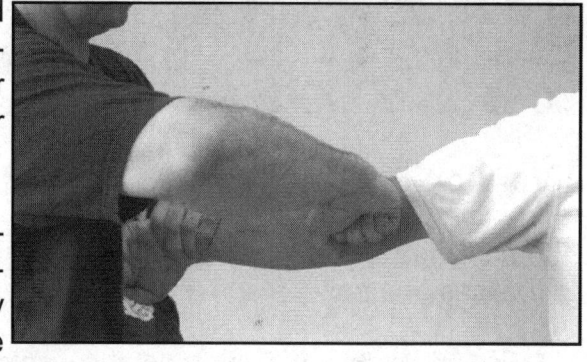

If suppression of the attacker rather than their destruction is our aim, we may be better suited to bring the palm to the opponent's elbow rather than hitting it.

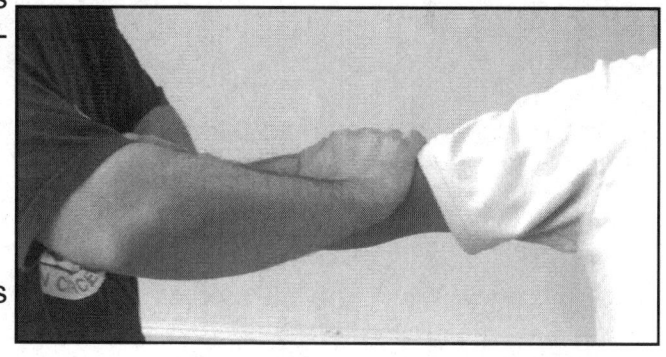

This doesn't change the practiced form, nor does it discard applications using fists, it just presents an alternative.

TCM: wrist points, TW11 Fire and Metal.

Version 5

In a grappling situation, our short hook punch takes on many of the qualities of a boxer's shovel hook.

This curves into the intercostal muscles and ribs and then back towards us slightly. We can imagine that this is like an ice-cream scoop.

On this occasion we choose to use the punch, as just a punch!

TCM: GB/LV crossing
Double wood.

Section 3
Performance

Bring your right foot briskly across your left ankle while looking to the left. The *kagezuki* remains in place.

The step is not completed until you are ready to. Do not just step across, but indicate the step and then place the foot, ensuring with inner-thigh muscle control that you maintain your balance all the way through.

The foot touches down and the step is rolled in, transferring your weight onto your right foot.

The left knee is raised high in front of your chest to the front. You should consider it as a *hizageri*, even though it appears to be preparation for the *fumikomi*.

The fumikomi is stamped for 98% of it's course, and the final 2% is placed onto the floor rather than dropped or thrust. This is a matter of control. The expansive technique is violent until it is controlled.

As the foot touches the floor, you simultaneously sink into *kibadachi* and bring the right arm directly up in a snapping motion that suggests the final position of *uchi-uke*.

Please note that the left hikite hand remains stationary throughout this sequence, and so there is no true uchi-uke as the right hand does not pass under the arm.

The only steps that occur in this kata are sideways.

While you may wish to step sideways in order to cover a large distance—say, in preparation for a side-kick while sparring—the primary reason that we use sideways steps is as a method of unbalancing an opponent.

You can try this as an exercise; take up a grappling position and try to move the other person when they don't wish to be moved. Dragging them around is hard work when you step to the left with the left foot.

However a small sideways step where you momentarily cross your ankles allows you to work from your centre when you try to move them.

Version 1

In this situation we have already closed to grappling distance.

We unite the sideways step with an arm action that looks just like kagezuki.
By lifting the attacker's elbow and

pushing it across our centre-line we effectively move to the outside line of his attacking zone.

Uniting this with a good hikite—pulling the hand back to the hip –we achieve a nice efficient piece of unbalancing.

It covers different planes and heights.

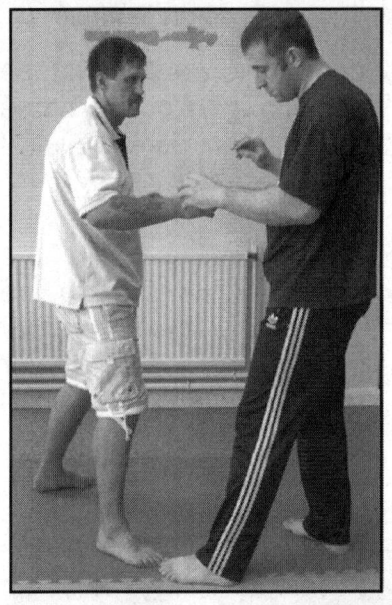

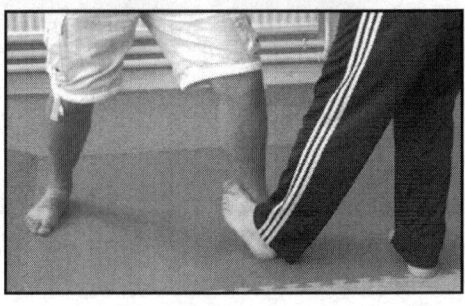

Sideways stepping attacks the ankle.

Should the attacker have the "wrong foot in front for the manoeuvre that we have chosen to do, we could

- Do a different technique
- Use their other leg ourselves—go in a different direction.
- Use our other leg—just change from the one shown here.
- Unbalance them so that they put the other foot in front
- Or simply step back so that the attacker is subliminally encouraged to step forwards to continue his aggression.

This then, would provide the ankle that we seek as our target.
The ankle itself is a wonderful target. We have very little regard for the safety of our own ankle—no inbuilt reflex twitches until it has already been hit. The area itself is delicate; the site of major nerves and blood passageways.

TCM: Sp6

Remembering that we want our hands to be properly engaged at the same time, the demonstration here is just of the cross step applied as a press to the ankle.

We can knock someone fully to the floor if the attack is taken in that direction instead of upwards or outwards. Think of a stamp instead of a sweep.

Of course this makes it even more brutal. I am reminded of a paramedic who was a Karate-ka telling me about a man who bled to death because an impact to the inside of his ankle had shattered the bone and ripped open the artery.

Once again we are talking about a technique that you do not use unless there is no other option.

Skilfully applied, this can be a great controlling technique without the need for damaging the structure of the attacker.

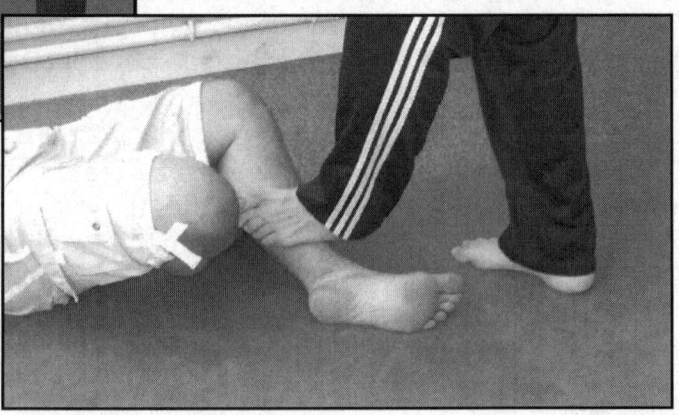

Version 2

However we have used the cross-step, we can see that wrenching the attacker's neck is going to be available to us.

Pulling on his hair, ears, or skin to secure his head, we can also pull on one of his arms by striking or abrasively contacting his arm to further disrupt his balance and control of the situation.

Our fist contacts the attacker's jaw as head is pulled on to the strike. Often, bringing the arms together can appear to strike, but we must also ask what could be in *between* those arms.

As we secure our position, the next set of movements clearly takes his head through multiple angles. We refer to this as "brain-stem twist", and it is highly disorienting, and in the most severe cases can be a neck-break.

Caution when working with your partner's health is mandatory.

TCM: PC6, ST4, Fire and Earth

Version 3

During any confrontation that isn't ended immediately there is likely to be a tustle. During this grappling situation we manage to get hold of the attacker.

With our hand already behind the attacker's head we can turn it over and gouge with the thumb knuckle, pushing down into his neck and causing him to buckle even further.

This gives us our next target as his face is turned.

Projecting our forearm back in means that we can strike with
- the forearm itself, into his face
- The elbow, down into his neck
- Or the fist, in an upper-cut type of motion.

The path that the fist takes will determine what is struck. Some people are mentally equipped for driving their knuckles into someone's jaw.

Others prefer to knead with their elbow as it feels more controlling, and allows for different levels of pain depending on the severity of the attack.

TCM: ST5, ST9, CV22 Earth

Section 4
Performance

This part of the kata should feel flowing, yet when viewed as photographs we find a staccato break-down.

From the previous "uchi-uke" position, you thrust your left fist out and bring your right fist to your left ear. Your right palm faces towards your head.

The hands are pulled in opposite directions, as the left hand is drawn towards the left ear, the right hand describes a gedan barai crossing to the outside edge of the body.

The left palm faces forwards.

From this point, the right hand comes up to a horizontal position as the left hand flies forward to strike.

The right hand is palm downwards and lies directly beneath the left elbow. The left palm is toward your face.

An issue arises over the use of hips to generate power in this portion of the kata in particular.

At no time must the knee be allowed to aim in a different direction to the foot, so in kiba dachi the opportunity for twisting the hips is much reduced.

That doesn't mean that the hips don't move, just that their movement is not allowed to prejudice the structure of the knees.

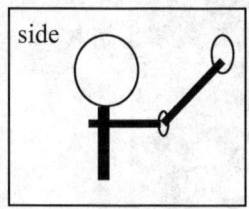

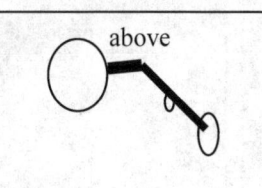

Here we can see another principle that we fall back on frequently.

Oyo principle: The idea of the "soft block" is that it is performed without tension. Tension in the muscle means that the muscle is pulling towards you. Arguably, none of our muscles push at all. Therefore tension will buckle your arm under enough pressure, and you can bet that the attacker will be intending for "enough pressure" to be there.

We measure out a lot of our martial arts in 45 degree angles. In soft blocking, we require our forearm to be 45 degrees up from horizontal, our bicep to be aligned 45 degrees away from the centre-line.

 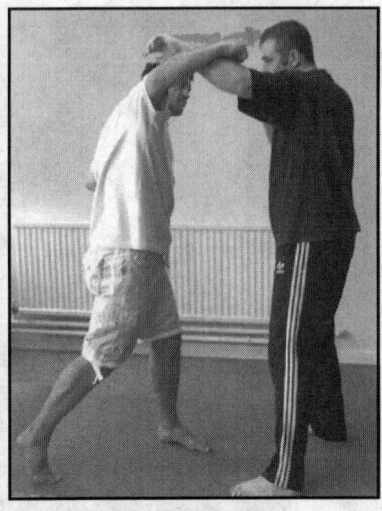

Version 1

In this example, we use soft block to stun the attacker, then continue to make contact with his arm as we cut underneath it with the radius.

Turning our body helps us to keep the torque against his arm and twists him so that we can deliver the uppercut retaliation.

TCM: TW11, ST4 Fire and Earth

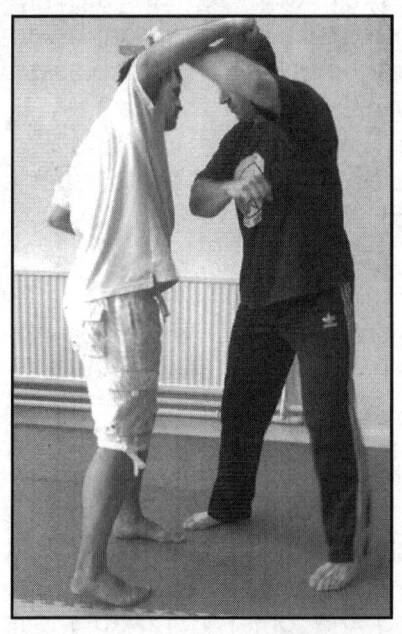

Version 2

The attacker comes in with his trusty round-house punch.

Soft-block can be used. But we can also sweep along the inside of the attacker's arm, opening up the intercostal muscles and ribs as a great target for a hammer-fist strike.

The human body is remarkably durable, and the ribs are constructed to allow for some compression. As the attacker has opened up that part of their body with their big hook, and we have added to that extension with the dragging motion, the ribs become highly susceptible to striking.

This stun allows us the time and the opponent's compliance to do the next part of the technique.

This is a strike to the brachio-radialis muscle of the forearm with a thumb-knuckle in a downward direction.

It causes the attacker to buckle forward.

At the same time we use the blocking arm to stay in contact and redirect the attacking arm back on itself.

The staying in contact part is vital, as it presses the attacker's crumpled arm across his body, preventing the use of that arm and causing the other hand to move away.

Our fist projecting past his arm to strike his face or throat.

The attacker's head has whipped forwards and then is shot backwards by our fist. We have increased the effectiveness of the strike by adding whiplash.

TCM: PC6, GB/LV crossing Fire and double Wood
LI10/11, ST4 Metal and Earth

Section 5
Performance

From the striking position.

Look to the left, then raise the left foot in front of the groin sharply—*nami gaeshi*—the returning wave.

As the foot touches the ground the arms are swung horizontally around to the left, maintaining their alignment. The left fist, however, rotates to face palm outwards.

Remember not to let the knees twist.

Look to the right, then raise the right foot in front of the groin sharply.

As the foot touches the ground, swing the arms horizontally around to the right, maintaining their alignment. However, return the left fist to the palm inwards position with a swift rotation.

This section then brings the hands to the hips in the *koshi gamae* position, the right fist is palm up as hikite, the left fist sits on top with the palm towards the body.

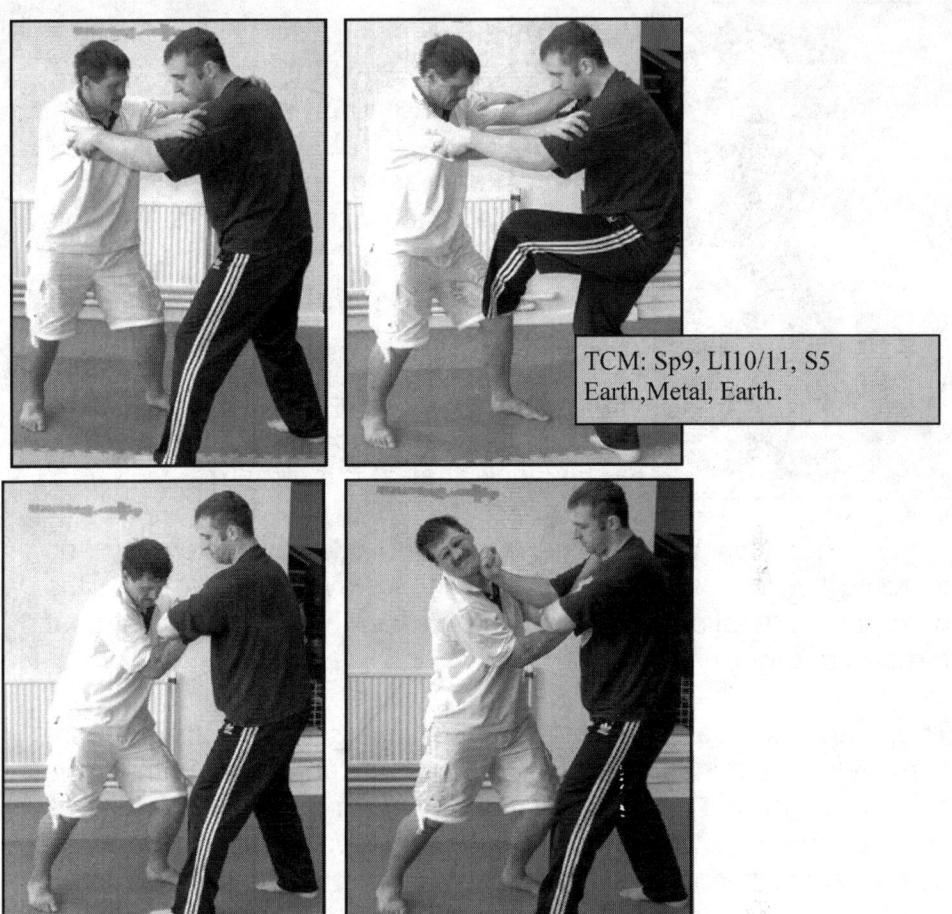

TCM: Sp9, LI10/11, S5
Earth,Metal, Earth.

Version 1

In this grappling situation we hit on multiple levels and multiple planes to gain the advantage. Hitting the inside of the thigh is much easier than striking the groin. It is much more available, very sensitive, and vulnerable to most types of retaliation. In this case we strike with the foot half-way up the inner thigh. We can even choose which leg to strike by jostling until the appropriate leg is in front. Results can vary from person to person, but the very least is that we have caused a distraction and gained compliance for the arms to do their work.

We use one arm to squeeze down and across the body to pull the attacker in, and then strike with the other arm.

Version 2

This choke is virtually invisible.

The attacker has grabbed us with both hands. We reach across his body for his right arm with our right arm, seizing at the elbow.

Pulling it back across our middle, we prevent him from following by grasping his collar as far back as we can reach, thus pressing his neck against our forearm.

If you unite this with any kind of footwork—by which I mean trapping his foot, his leg; or kicking them away as we do in the nami-gaeshi application—then his bodyweight hangs against your forearm and grab.

There are various arguments against using chokes that secure themselves against clothing—the usual one being that the attacker might not be wearing a shirt and that modern clothing is not as sturdy as the training uniform. We can tell you quite certainly that this can be performed against someone wearing a vest, and with a little more skill/ training against someone with no top on.

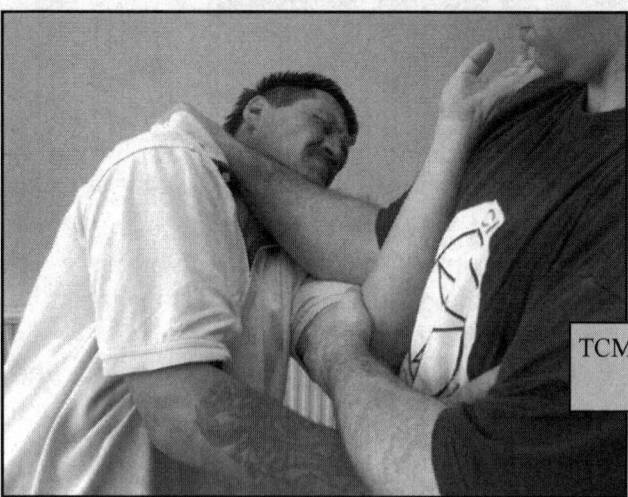

TCM: HT3, LI18 Fire and Metal

Version 3

It should be no surprise that many of our applications deal with a right hook. It is the most common of assault weapons. Regardless of nationality or era, the right hook is prominent.

Once again, if presented with a hook punch, we can try to gain the outside line by deflecting it over the top of us and downwards, disabling further punches from the attacker.

Changing hands to maintain contact, our parrying arm snakes around the attacker's neck, squeezing towards us even as we push the jugular and windpipe sideways. The human body is remarkably resistant to compression, but tearing and shearing motions are effective, especially when combined with compression.

TCM: LI10/11, PC6, LU5, LI18, ST9. Metal, Fire, Earth

We then reinforce this by bringing our elbow down into the attacker's shoulder, giving them pain that stops them from resisting the choke.

This covering of the choking arm with another arm is a good tactic. The attacker's first instinct is to free their throat. In doing so they will reach up and grab. The arm that is available to them for release is not the one that is actually causing the choke, and as such they are not actually liberating themselves even if they do pull the arm away.

Put another way; the inner hand is the one doing the work, and it is shielded by the outer hand.

TCM: LU1

Version 4

In a variation on the above technique, we receive a straight punch by moving off to the side and parrying. We then bring our arm down across their elbow, causing them to bend their arm inwards away from us. This makes it much less likely that they can effectively use their other hand.

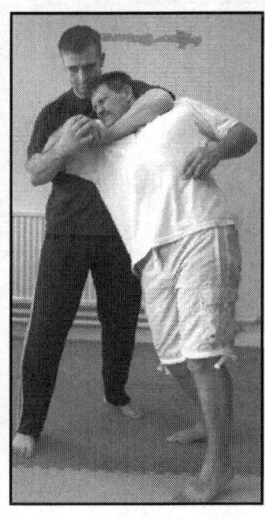

We effect a wrist lock by bending their arm in and pinning in place with an arm that goes around the back of the attacker and makes any resistance on their part worse for their neck. It reinforces the choke.

Push down on their elbow to cause a great compression of the attacker's wrist.
Continued...

 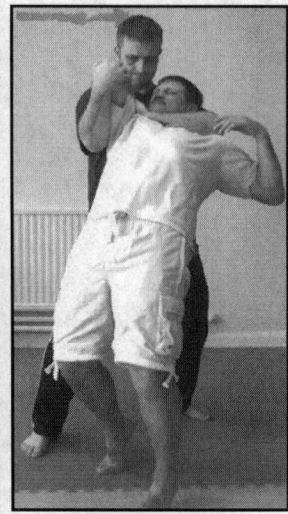

Now the attacker's own arm is locking our arm against their throat.

We have the attacker's wrist supported not just by our hand, but also by pressing it back towards our own body.

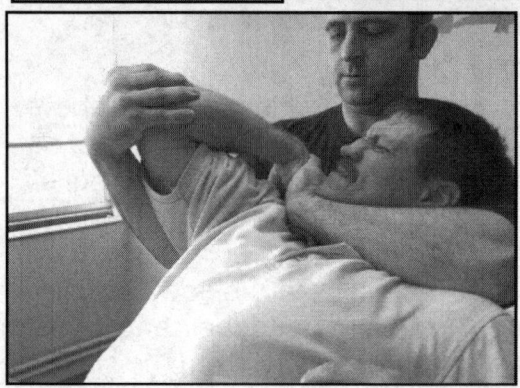

TCM: HT/SI, LI3, ST9 Fire, Metal, and Earth

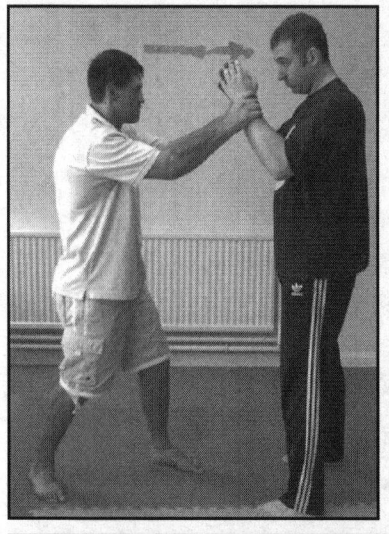

Version 5

In this situation our wrists have been grabbed as the attacker tries to force us backwards or prevent us from striking their face.

There are many ways that we can pull out of this grasp, but we might be better suited to clasping their hand to our arm and twisting our arms together.

As we twist, the attacker's natural instinct is to slip off as we collide our elbow with theirs. By understanding the pre-determined response we can turn their reaction into something that gives them pain.

This is achieved by keeping their hand attached to us.

Continued...

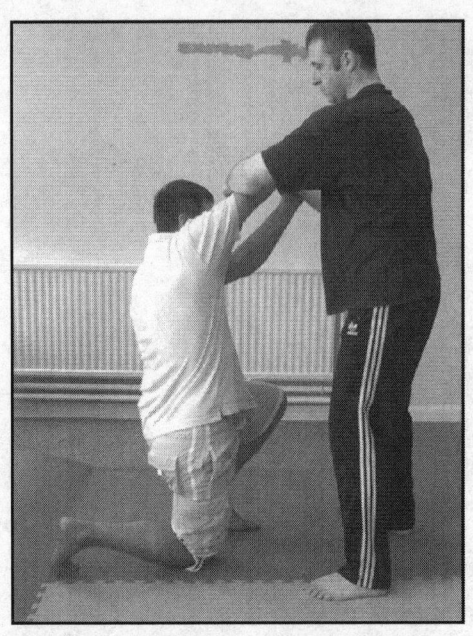

Essentially, it is a wrist-lock that drives them to the floor.

We place our arm between the attacker's forearm and their bicep and we effect a fair bit of leverage.

With a turn of our hand, just as the kata has us perform, we have a further option for wrist locks with their hand.

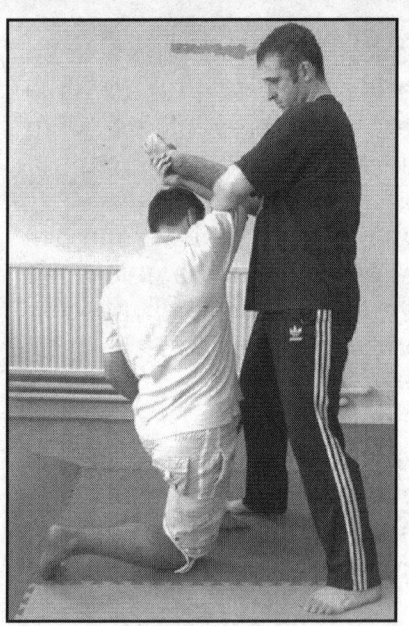

TCM: wrist points, TW11, LI3, LI10/11 Fire and Metal

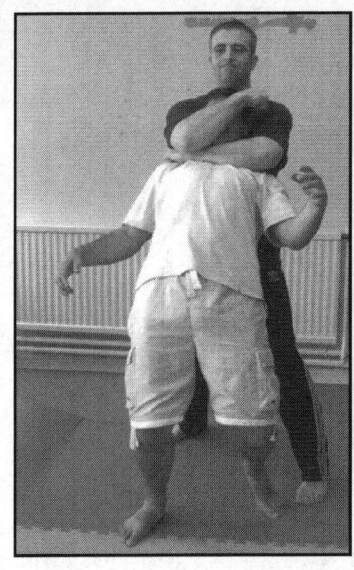

Version 6

When we think about locks and takedowns, it is quite natural to think about the human skeletal system and the joints. Barring usually works because we lock out one joint against itself and thereby cause pain.

In this instance we deflect any incoming attack and seek a position behind the attacker.

Achieving the choke that we have looked at previously, on this occasion we have failed to utilise the attackers wrists for any kind of lock.

We simply grind our forearm against his face.

Preferably, we get our styloid process against their opposite eyebrow and simply squeeze towards our chest. Wherever our arm happens to contact will be fine, the face is a very sensitive area and we are grinding the nerves against the hard skull beneath.

A face bar hurts a lot, and is mostly not thought of by martial artists or aggressors as we're not pressuring joints.

TCM: LI21, ST5 Metal & Earth

Version 7

A straightforward explanation for this move has the attacker grab our lapels.

By doing this the attacker has set up his twin forearms (and especially the brachioradialis) for retaliation. Bringing our forearm down upon them we buckle his arms.

We can actually choose our target for striking. If you bring your forearm down more heavily upon one arm or the other you will observe different turns of the attacker's head.

Our strike can be an upper-cut to the jaw, or a fist to the throat, or a downward strike upon the cheekbone, temple, or eye. Or you can just pulverise the nose, but you should beware, as just breaking noses might produce blood, but often the attacker can fight on.

We seek to stun them more thoroughly than that.

TCM: LI10/11, ST9, ST5, ST1
Metal & Earth

Version 8

Here we can see that we have evaded and parried a straight punch—in this case a jab– and darted past the opponent. We take a hand over the top of their attack to strike against his neck. Using our forearm and bicep we then secure him and pull down so that his back is arched over. This utilises the *leave no gap* rule and looks at the performance position, asking "what's the purpose of the gap, then?"

In this case, we have decided to illustrate the gap as containing the upper quarters of the attacker.

TCM: SI/HT, ST/LI, LU1 Fire, Earth, and Metal

Version 9

If we manage to negotiate a position behind the attacker by pulling and changing their balance, and by using the BAR tactics that we are aware of, then we can wrench on their neck from this angle too.

We pull their head backwards and down while striking into the jaw with the thumb knuckle directed towards ourselves. This can also be used to knead the attacker's jaw to gain further compliance.

Taking the hand past their face, we try to maintain contact with their head for as long as possible en route.

Should we lose our grip then we can choose to bump our forearm against the attacker's neck. Just the thrust forward along the line of the neck can be jarring.

Of course, if we take our hand forward and retain contact with the attacker's head then we will damage the attacker's neck.

Continued...

> TCM: ST4, GB cluster, GV, ST6, ST1-3 Earth, Wood

Then we push our hands back towards a central position, achieving a reverse of the choke, and use our descending forearm to strike into the neck.

This type of attack means that the whole of our forearm contacts their head. We will also hit vulnerable areas on the face.

If by chance the attacker's head was spun so far that they began to fall forward, then it becomes possible for us to inject our elbow towards their core with the same follow-up movement, ensnaring their arm instead of their neck with or "restraining" hand.

TCM: BL Water

Version 10

Face to face with the attacker, we can strike to the back of the neck, or just clasp as in a grappling hold.

We pull the attacker's head down towards us, and then strike directly into the trapezius with our elbow, in the direction of their opposite foot.

Again we are directed to note that the fist is not necessarily the weapon of choice, and the kata might seem to hide the real application.

Truthfully, the application is there for all to see, if you can look past the descriptive terminology that is used to name the moves in the solo re-enactment of the combat.

TCM: SI15

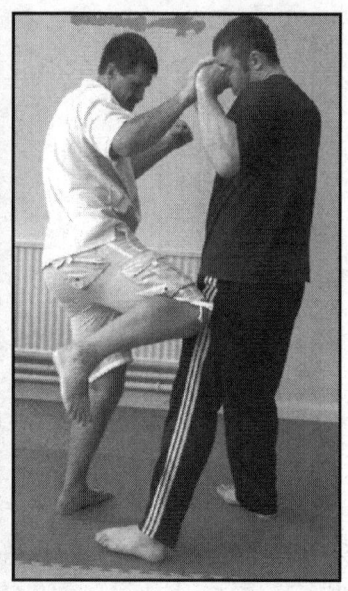
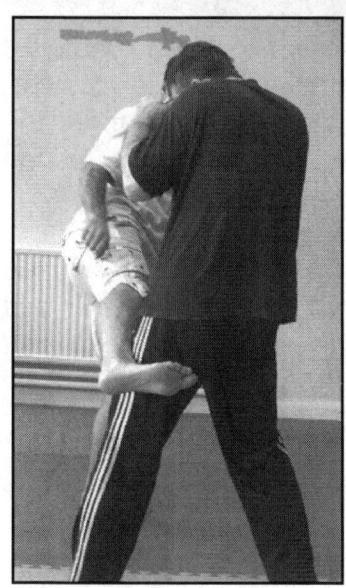

Taking a look at the nami gaeshi, we might use it defensively against a kick.

For it to be used to block a kick and fit our criteria for effective use of kata movement, it has to be usable against a commonly occurring method of attack.

Now, the types of kick that we are likely to meet outside the dojo fall into two broad categories, the sweeping kick and the round kick.

We are unlikely to meet a maegeri—front kick—as practised in the dojo.

With a little bit of positioning, we can use the same block against both, but we'll use the round kick in our example.

The good thing about kicks is that they take a little bit longer to arrive than most punches. There aren't too many ex-pert kickers who aren't martial artists.

The bad news is that a great lop-ing kick can be extremely power-ful. We are talking about the biggest muscles in the human body, and the biggest bones.

With a bit of good timing, we see the kick hefted and raise our foot out of the way, projecting our knee into the course of the kick, impaling it.

Our ideal targets are on the inside of the thigh, but if we hap-pen to catch the top of the thigh this can be destructive, too.

Whenever we are letting our legs perform a technique, it is vital that our hands are engaged in something too. At the very least they are held high to protect our upper areas while our leg is protecting our lower areas.

Section 6
Performance

Having made the *koshi gamae*—hip guard—posture, we get to the first *kiai*—spirit shout—with this single technique.

The *yumi zuki*—bow punch—looks as though one has drawn an arrow back through the bow, yet the action to perform it is quite different.

Described as a punch, there is a certain circularity to the movement that makes the left fist (in this case) more like a hammer-fist strike than anything else.

The technique is executed without any noticeable change in stance, and is the focus of the kiai.

Version 1

The attacker attempts a great swinging hook punch. Instinctively we apply our trained soft-block. Following the motion of the punch we allow it to settle against us and then latch it and pull the attacker onto our projected fist as it goes sideways to their jaw.

TCM: PC6, LU, LI, ST4-6 Fire, metal, and Earth

Version 2

The attacker's hook get's blocked with our soft block, once again.

This time we find ourselves stepping into the attack in a slightly more circular way.

In a reverse of the previous technique we pull their attacking arm forwards and bring our forearm or elbow into their jaw.

Because we are on the inside of this attack we need to pull decisively and strike decisively to avoid being struck by his other hand.

Partly, we rely upon cross-body motor reaction.

TCM: PC, LI, S4-6. Fire, Metal, Earth

TCM: SI, HT, LI, LU. ST4-6
Fire and Metal

Version 3

Parrying off a straight, we arrange ourselves on the "outside" line in this example. Making constant contact with the attacker's arm allows us to identify his location without the benefit of processing what we see.

Our initial contact is a block/parry, but the secondary contact is trained to be more receptive and we are able to pull on the attacking hand.

Then we simply punch over the top of it.

Version 4

Taking the same situation, in this case we project under the attacker's arm.

This is noteworthy because the body is more primed for being damaged when the arm is raised and pulled, as mentioned previously with the intercostal muscles.

The second reason why this might be a better target is that the head is effectively sitting on a spring and will recoil when struck. While this can be damaging in itself, the body is committed to it's location by the weight-bearing foot, but also by the grabbing hand.

TCM: wrist points, GB/LV crossing, Fire, Metal, Double Wood.

Version 5

By pulling the attacking hand past us and closing the distance we can reverse the situation once more and see how the elbow becomes the striking weapon.

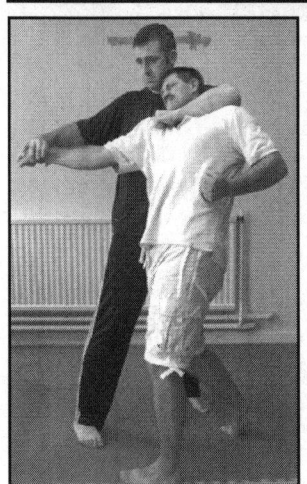 

TCM: Wrsit points, ST9, LI18
Metal, Fire, and Earth

Version 6

As the attacker tries his cross again, we parry and slide to the outside. This time we manage to get further round, behind them.

We cause the attacker a problem when we pull on their attacking arm and bring our "hook punch" from behind them as a choke.

Once again we see that the motion of securing a choke looks more like a punch as it does not swing out and back again, but rather rips right along the neck.

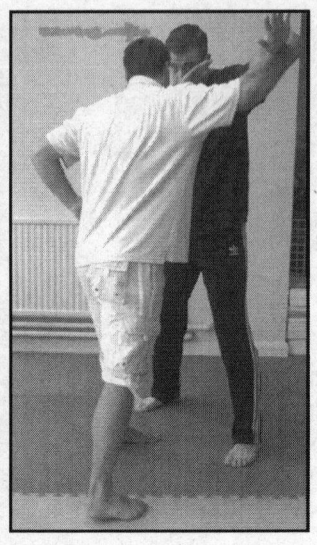

Version 7

As the attacker swings his roundhouse attack, we move in the same direction as the force of his blow—riding it without physically stopping it.

As we move we can use that same direction of travel to loop a short hook punch back to the attacker's jaw.

Latching the attacker's wrist will also help to destabilise them and bring the head down to a manageable height.

We are open to a continued attack, so we need to make sure that there is some shock in the block and no time delay between moving and hitting back..

TCM: LU, LI, ST4-6. Fire, Metal, and Earth

Version 8

On this occasion we receive the hook in our trained fashion and latch onto the attacking arm, pulling it as we do.

Moving in we project the elbow into the ribs again.

If it is at all possible, it is useful to hyperextend the attacker's elbow and pull away from the attacker's power zone with the manner that we grip, during this move.

TCM: wrist points,, GB/LV crossing. Fire, Metal, Wood

Version 9

If we are long enough in the arm then we have more options when someone grabs our throat.

The simplest method of extrication is hit the insides of the attacker's wrists, one straight after the other, working right to right and left to left.
Just hitting them or just kicking them may be available to us, but not necessarily, so it's wise to have options.

The natural reaction is actually not that clever, pulling on the arms from the outside to prise them apart. It works against the natural laws of the body pulling towards the centre. We need to train out the ordinary reaction in favour of one that will save us.

In this instance we pull on one of the attacker's wrists in that manner and turn our body slightly sideways. This allows us a bit more breathing space.

TCM: wrist points, LI18, ST9
Fire, Metal, Earth

Keeping the downward pressure on the attacker's arm, we thrust our fist directly towards his throat.

Version 10

An attacker can be guided as to how they will hit us by how wide our "guard" or "fence" is.

A narrow guard will subconsciously programme them towards round punches, whereas a wide guard will lead them to strike "down the middle".

If we are confident enough, we can tempt the attacker towards the middle and then position ourselves to push past them.

We could just run, from there.

If the situation is more desperate then we can latch and bring our other hand back in as a strike, choke, or face bar/neck wrench.

TCM: wrist points, ST4-6, LI21, Fire, Metal, Earth.

So we can see that there are a huge number of variations available to us.

Section 7

Performance

Following the kiai, our left hand shoots across underneath the right hand, and then opens out slowly while the right hand pulls back, hikite. It is customary to use this move to regain the breath and renew the concentration for the second half of the performance.

Then we slam the elbow to the waiting hand, and...

Yes, the rest of the moves are the same as the ones that came before, but with right and left reversed.

And after the second yumizuki and kiai, you return to *yame*—finish.

Look to the front, slowly lower the hands and retract the right foot to bring the feet together.

The hands open and resume their initial position.

You should remain aware and ready. Don't think of yame as relax, rather think of it as "return to the beginning". Naore is relax.

And we haven't mentioned...

We've looked at all of these applications, and I've left out something absolutely crucial to understanding this kata.

The Stance.

That position, the horse-riding stance, is the most vital piece of application going. It is the use of bodyweight in the application. The front stance represents pushing the bodyweight forward. The back stance represents resistance and pulling while applying a technique.

The one that this kata consists of represents the idea of dropping the body down. No matter how great your best technique is, it can only be better with bodyweight applied.

Look back again at all of the applications that you see within this book. What you will find is that I have rarely had to drop into a full kibadachi. That's deliberate, honestly.

The reason for this is that the techniques I am applying work very well, and that as I have conducted them on Richard I have achieved the desired result for the sake of the photo without too much physical strength. This is something that you work towards, but do not rely on.

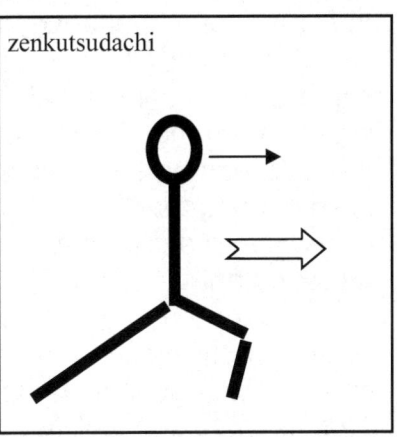

zenkutsudachi

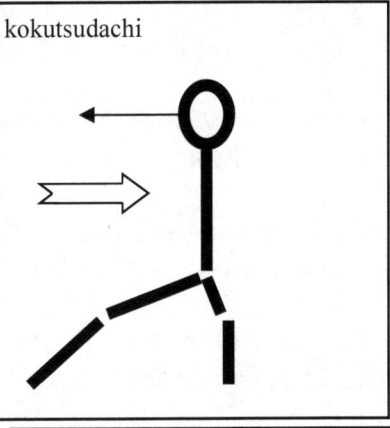

kokutsudachi

kibadachi

I am large, and began training in Karate in the early 80's, that's a fair bit of experience. That doesn't mean that everyone studying Tekki Shodan or referencing this book will have the same or more—most will have a lot less. Most people will be smaller than me. The techniques need to work for everyone, so the kata has us throw everything we can into the moves. This is something that when it comes to the crunch and you throw in everything that you have, is a vital part of making it work to the fullest extent.

When practising the kata solo, we sit low in kibadachi, in the sure knowledge that under stress I may only be able to use 50% of my total ability. Therefore that 50% must be *good enough*. Train your body to produce 200% of what you will require, then the 100% that comes out under stress will be right.

Hence—low stance, control of the body, distinct visualisation, bodyweight applied downwards.

The kata has us move sideways. We can take this to indicate that the attacker should be moved sideways. We can take it to show that we should adopt a side-on posture, but more than anything else, the horse-riding stance is about dropping your body downwards.

Conclusions

So there you have Tekki Shodan. The first part of the family. You will see from parts two and three that Shodan is very important. The relationship with the other two parts needs a lot of thought.

I've shown you the kata as it's performed—and those pictures were taken in 2001. I hope I perform it a bit better, now. We've shown the applications, which you must understand have a slightly exploded view as the action really takes place in very close proximity. You've seen moves performed from all manner of attacks, and yet a book can't really show you how those things work in motion.

Still, if they made you think about oyo—application - then I can say we've spurred your study on. I'd urge you to try the moves with restraint, and only build up the activity level as you understand what the moves do.

..And only ever work up to your training partner's pain threshold. Never what you think they can take, always start low and put a little more in rather than having to try to put less in.

Come and see us at seminars and at my dojo. Sincere learners are always welcome. We can discuss the bits that didn't make sense, as different people grasp the information in different ways.

I started out by saying that this book is about kata. It's about what you consider kata practice to be. Nine years is a long time to just be stomping about in Kibadachi. As long as that time includes the preparation of the mind and the body and forging *both* through systematic trials that give meaning to the shapes that the body throws, then it has more intricacy.

Too often we rush to learn the moves to pass a grade. We learn for the sake of collecting without ever really *knowing*. That's why the masters of old said that you only ever need two or three kata—they would know them inside and out.

Within my own association I constantly urge newly qualified brown belts to go back and take a deeper look at Tekki. We posit that the 4th kyu students don't have enough time to understand Tekki properly. Some say that they should wait until they understand it before they can wear the brown belt, but nine years is a long time as a 4th kyu. Competent beginners; the shodan black belts, now *they* should have a good grasp of what Tekki is all about.

As Tekki is not regarded as a particularly pretty kata by most people, it isn't used to win many competitions. The moves within it aren't very spectacular to look at in demonstration/competition. Kata with jumping and spinning and nekoashi dachi are much more popular for aesthetic competitors. For these reasons Tekki gets sidelined in competition oriented clubs in favour of more dynamic and acrobatic performances. Clubs that dwell on sport have very little use for Tekki except as a leg strengthening exercise.

Tekki should be regarded in Shotokan as the heart of the art, just as Sanchin is regarded in Gojuryu. Picture Funakoshi, stood aloft his house in a storm, holding a tatami above his head to test the power of his legs in kibadachi. For something inconsequential? No.

Anthony Blades renshi has shown me that what I thought was a hard-hitting piece of work is actually about circularity. He has shown that the movements can still be fluid, even locked into this virtually static form. In him I can see why some people claim that Tekki is related to the Crane family of kata.

This puts it's origins in the hands of the Chinese martial arts. There is, however, no single Chinese pattern/form that reflects this one. The Okinawan proclivity for using fists where Chinese arts use open hands is another factor in the changes that have occurred.

Tekki ends up being something that you either love or loath. I think that it deserves a lot more attention than it gets in many grading syllabi. It's truly a method of fighting—a set of principles that lead you to a system you can rely on.

That is, if it's given the proper study.

Appendices

Tekki Shodan

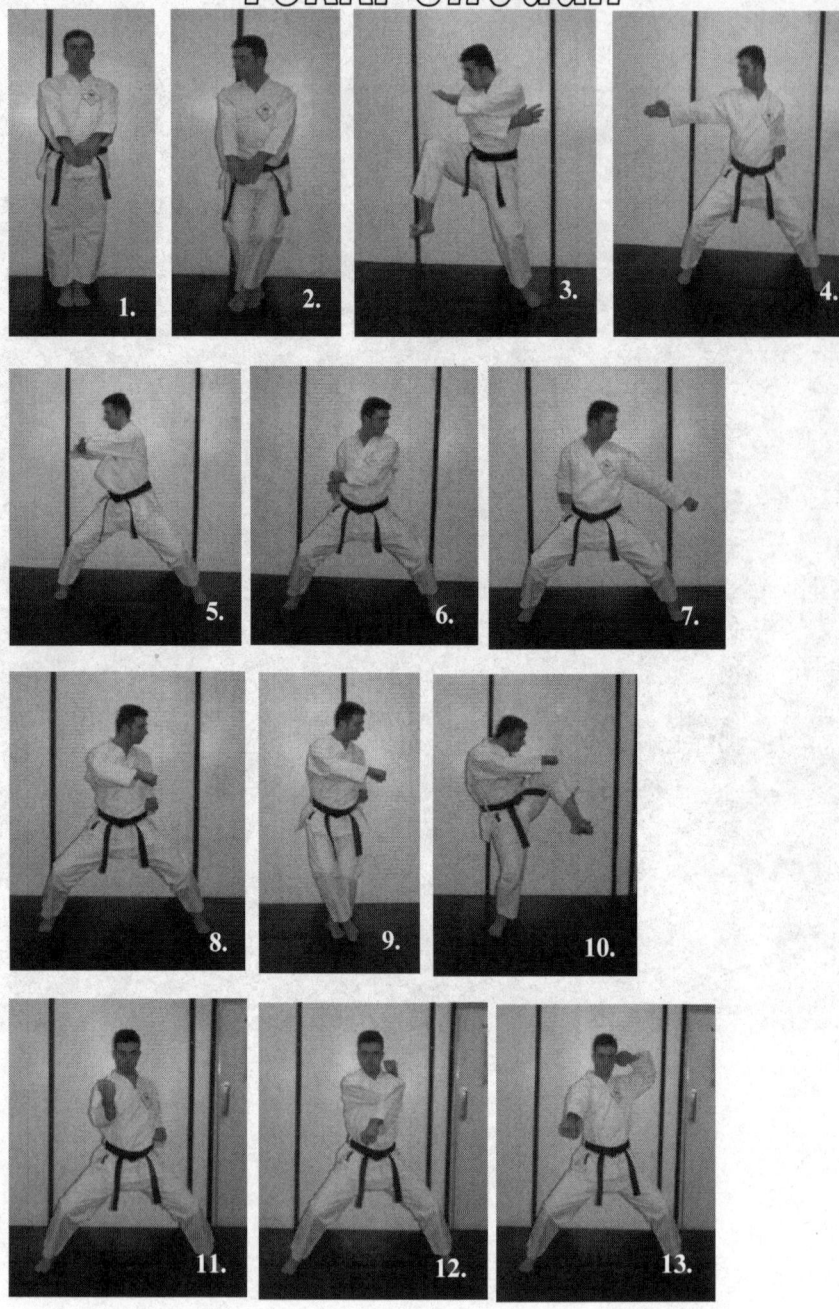

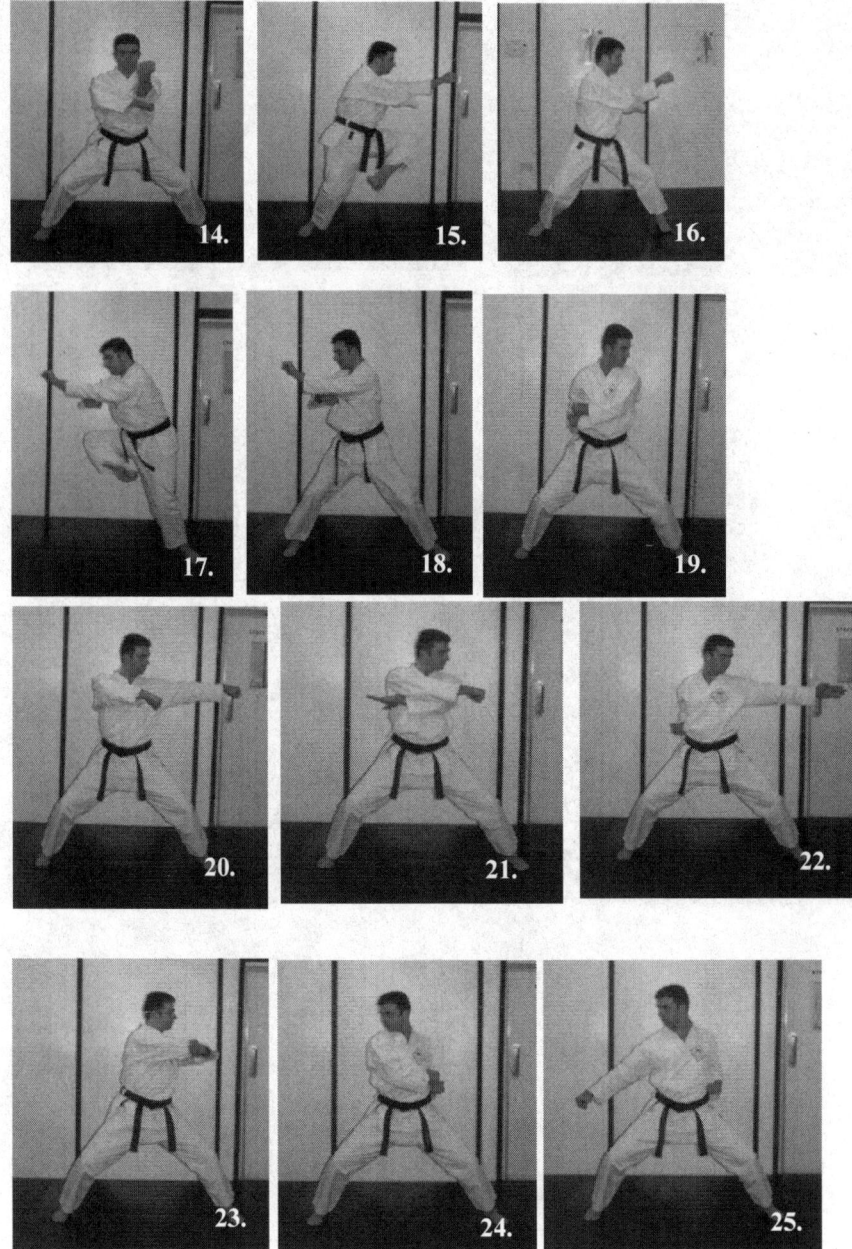

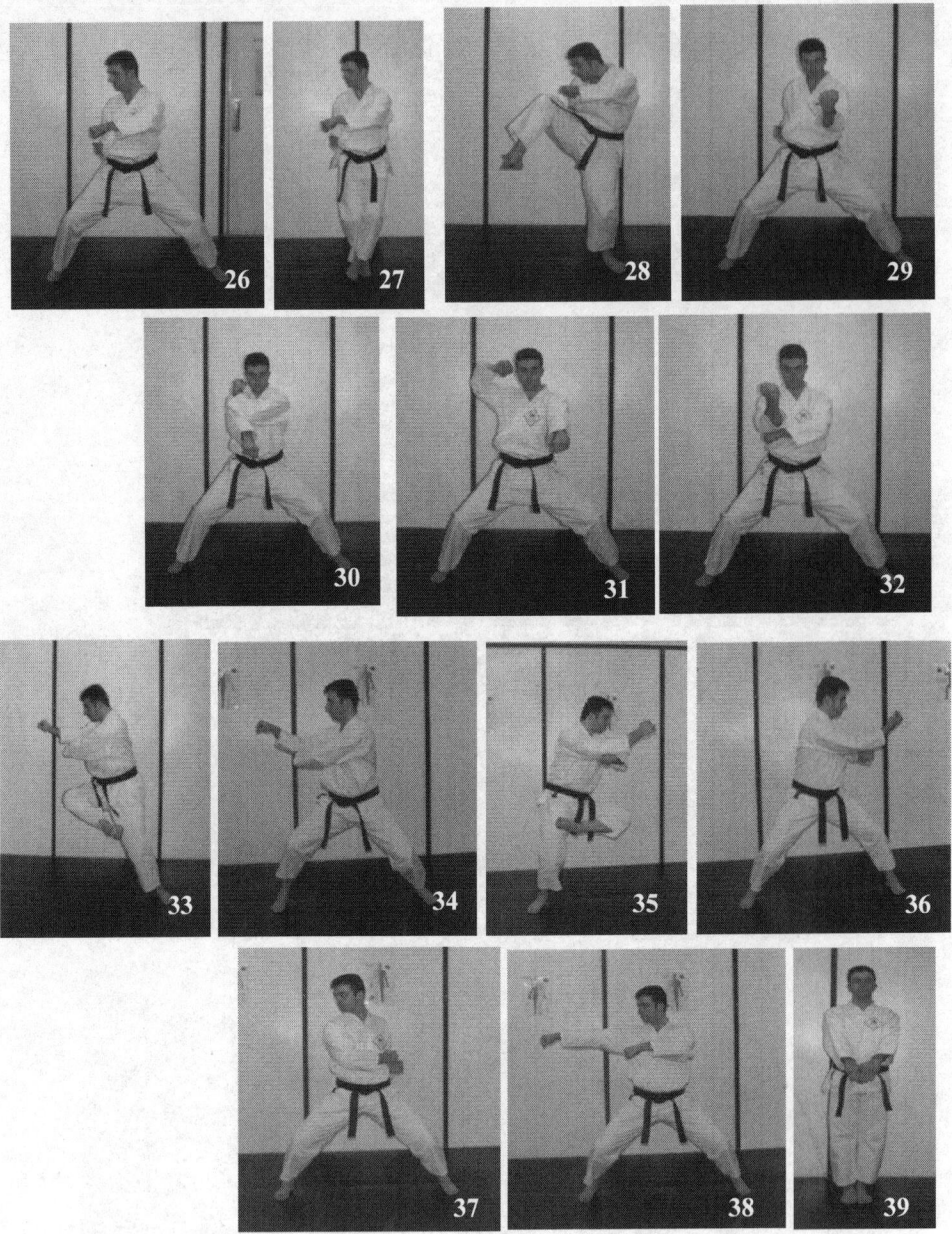

Oyo Principle: we do not begin by standing in any stance but the natural one, with one foot slightly in front of the other.

Oyo Principle: go through what is or is not justified in your mind a long time before any conflict actually comes. There isn't much time for decision making when in front of an attacker.

Oyo Principle: the further from the base of the joint pressure is exerted, the less strength is needed. It's leverage.

Oyo Principle: cross body motor reaction stops the other hand from being used immediately.

Oyo Principle: when we move backwards as a flinch reaction we channel the action into something useful.

Oyo Principle: If possible, seek the outside line, seek the "blindside".

Oyo Principle: The balance is affected by multi-directional effort.

Oyo principle: redundancy. Even if the technique doesn't go to the exact location we want, it will still serve.

Oyo Principle: the opponent crossing the centreline involuntarily confuses them momentarily. It's why we don't cross our hands on the steering wheel.

Oyo Principle: Having made contact, we maintain contact.

Oyo principle: The idea of the "soft block" is that it is performed without tension. Tension in the muscle means that the muscle is pulling towards you. Arguably, none of our muscles push at all. Therefore tension will buckle your arm under enough pressure, and you can bet that the attacker will be intending for "enough pressure" to be there.

We measure out a lot of our martial arts in 45 degree angles. In soft blocking, we require our forearm to be 45 degrees up from horizontal, our bicep to be aligned 45 degrees away from the centre-line.

As you can see, the principles that are mentioned early in the book are all appropriate for **all** the applications. There are a lot more besides. But these are the ones that seemed *most* relevant.

The most important thing is to try to avoid the combat situations in the first place—that's winning for real. It's only when our awareness slips that situations can become dangerous, and that's where our training is needed.

Karate instructors often count with the words ichi, ni, san, chi, and goh for 1-5 in Japanese, but the kata are not named the same way.

Interestingly, *Shodan* means First level, but *Nidan* means Level Two. *Sandan* is Level Three, *Godan* is Level Five, but *Yondan* is Fourth Level.
This has to do with good manners in not naming something (a kata in this case) with something that sounds like the Japanese word for "death". So *Chidan* become *Yondan*, and *Shichidan* (Level Seven) becomes *Nanadan* (Seventh Level). Shodan rather than Ichidan is because we have first instead of one—like beginning (shoshin—beginners' mind).

I was told this by a Japanese instructor. A visitor to my dojo from Osaka said that she had never heard such nonsense.

Terminology

Age uke rising receiver
Bunkai analysis
Chudan middlelevel
Dan post-black belt grades
Embusen performance line
Funakoshi Gichin the name of the founder of Shotokan
Gedan barai low level sweep
Godan level 5
Hanmi half-on
Heian Peace
Hidari left
Hikite returning hand
Itosu Ankoh the teacher of master Funakoshi
Kage zuki hook punch (lit. "key-shape" punch)
Kake hooking
Karate do The way of the Empty Hand
Kata form
Kiai everything together
Kibadachi horse-riding stance
Kihon basics
Kokutsudachi back stance

Koshi gamae hip guard/posture
Kyu pre-black belt grades.
Migi right
Muchimi sticking
Naore/enoi relax
Nekoashi dachi cat-foot stance
Nidan level 2
Oizuki lunge thrust
Oyo application
Sandan level 3
Satori enlightenment
Shodan level one
Shomen the front
Shoshin beginners' mind
shotokan The Hall of "Pine Waves"
Shuto uke sword hand receiver
Tatami straw mat
Tettsui uchi hammerfist strike
Uchiuke inside receiver technique
Uraken uchi backfist strike
Urazuki uppercut (lit. back of punch)
Yamae return to ready position
Yoi ready
Yondan fourth level
Yumizuki "bow" punch
Zenkutsudachi front stance

The Cosmology of the Tekki kata

The basic shape made by the first Tekki kata reflects the line "-".

This represents the number "1" in Japan. It was said that hand-writing experts could foretell the future of a client from how the brushed the character — on parchment with ink. The simplicity and purity of the line was said to show an awful lot about someone.

This kata has a step to the right as it's first move, yet the left foot does the step. You will recall that the left foot takes the first step in most of the kata, especially the Heian kata which precede this one in most syllabi.

As noted earlier, there are three Tekki kata. The number three is significant to the Oriental superstition. In no way should the word superstition be construed negatively, it is just a description of a way of thought beyond the common Occidental mindset.

Mind body spirit
Heaven man earth
Mind breath body
Shu ha ri.

The true reason for the distinction into three kata can never be known. There are no books telling us what the founders of these kata originally intended. There is only cultural context and background knowledge for us to make educated guesses from.

Kata as Meditation

As the *jutsu* forms of karate became popularised as *do* forms, theoretically, the object of training changed. Funakoshi sensei's idea was that Karate would be treated as *moving meditation* for the betterment of character. Yet the majority of those taking part could only see the older fighting method, and so the art became a split personality. It only gets worse when you consider that the term *do* has been cast in the public perception as relating to sport based arts, when the Chinese term *Tao* (meaning the same thing) is seen as being spiritual.

術

jutsu

The idea that you can lose yourself in the performance of kata is laudable, and something that all practitioners should try. Some will argue that this method prevents fighting applications from being made part of the subconscious, but we would argue that it internalises the movements to the ultimate degree, leading the martial arts practitioner back to the idea of "becoming the movement" instead of "doing the movement". Isn't this one of Bruce Lee's maxim's—"*Don't think, feel.*"?

道

do

Kata performed hard and fast become internalised as combative movements which flow together.

気

Kata performed slowly and with the *idea* of fostering greater **ki** become a form of what-the-Chinese call "*Chi-Gung*". That is a life-enhancing exercise for healthy body and internal energy.

ki

In today's society, when we have so much to worry about, and so many things wrong with the world, there is very little that can totally absorb us. Distractions abound. Maybe, just maybe, you can lose yourself for a time in training. It helps if that training has a pre-arranged form, something that you can just repeat, mindful of movement and betterment, yet slipping from being totally conscious. The Japanese have a word for the flash of inspiration and enlightenment that can be visited upon us at these times—SATORI.

悟

satori

There's no better way to leave you than that.

About the author

John Burke began training in Karate in 1981. He has had breaks in his training which has led to investigations into Aikido, and Taekwondo, but eventually led him back to Karate.

He has had a fortunate selection of teachers, always with what he needed at each point in his training, from the purely physical to the realistic, from the spiritual to the sporting.

John's first book, **Fortress Storming**, concentrated on the Bassai Dai kata and its applications, and was well received by

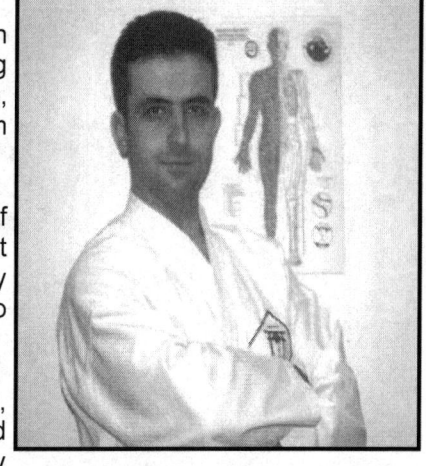

martial artists. Also available are his applications to the Heian/Pinan series of Kata **Peaceful Mind**; the beginners guide, **A Karate Primer**, and the book on the grading **Syllabus**.

Nowadays, John has featured in articles for *Martial Arts Illustrated and Traditional Karate* magazines and spends his time teaching Karate and Iaido, writing books and making tuition dvds.

His seminars are taught across Britain and internationally, and his students have clubs that form the Eikoku Karate-do Keikokai— an association dedicated to training incorporating the old ways.

A large amount of information is available from John's website, as are his other products, at
www.thebunkaiguy.com

Seminars with John Burke sensei are available internationally to cover

Traditional Karate,
Kata Bunkai,
Oyo,
and Pressure Points.

For more information contact **01626 360 999**
E-mail sensei@karateacademy.co.uk

Website www.karateacademy.co.uk

Video & DVD footage of tuition and seminars also available.

2007 Grading group

Regular training in the **Eikoku Karatedo Keikokai** under John Burke and his team of instructors can be undertaken across Devon

First two lessons are free. New members receive a free uniform upon joining. One fee covers training at all venues.

For an up to date list of venues and times in **Newton Abbot, Totnes, and Torquay**, please see our website.

Also Available

Involving the same author.

Books:

Fortress Storming. Examining the Bassai Dai kata, performance, and applications

Peaceful Mind. Examining the Heian kata, performance and applications.

Grading Syllabus. The official syllabus for the Eikoku Karate-do Keikokai. Listing all the basics, Kumite, Kata, and Oyo that must be learned and providing guidance on Bunkai requirements for examinations.

A Karate Primer. Background, History, Philosophy, and sample applications for Karate practice.

Fortress Storming—the Minor Version. Examining the performance and applications of the Bassai Sho kata.

DVDs

Syllabus dvds for the Eikoku Karate-do Keikokai for each grade:
White Belt
Orange Belt
Red Belt
Yellow Belt
Green Belt
Purple Belt
Purple & White Belt
Brown Belt
Brown—Brown & White Belt
Brown & Double White Belt

Seminar series
Nijushiho & Niseishi Kata Comparison

OCI 2003 double disc set.

Kata Application series
Kihon
Heian Shodan
Heian Nidan
Heian Sandan
Heian Yondan
Heian Godan
Tekki Shodan
Bassai Dai
Jion

Call 01626 360999 to order, or see
www.thebunkaiguy.com

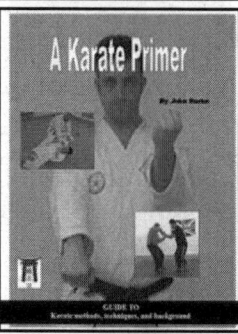

Resources

Rather than a bibliography, I find that people provide more feedback and information. While good books are a great resource, good people can never be replaced. The number of books and articles that I have drawn reference from are innumerable, but the people who influence our development are easier to list:

Eikoku Karate-do Keikokai

This is the organisation of our karate, where application plays a major part in learning kata. The members are a terrific source of encouragement and inspiration, and without them this book would not exist.
The association is open to clubs to join, but potential instructors must be willing to be inspected and approved prior to membership being granted.
Information: www.karateacademy.co.uk
Association enquiries: info@karateacademy.co.uk
Training enquiries: sensei@karateacademy.co.uk
01626 360999

Russell Stutely

The renown pressure point expert and founder of OCFM. Russell has a wealth of information and was responsible for the technology that put the pieces of the puzzle together in my head.
www.russellstutely.co.uk

Patrick McCarthy

Hanshi McCarthy is a valuable resource for the world of martial arts. His historical research and publications are groundbreaking. Without him much knowledge would not have come to light.
Hanshi is the founder of the International Ryukyu Karate-jutsu Research Society.
www.koryu-uchinadi.com
KSL—The discussion forum of the International Ryukyu Karate-jutsu Research Society. The members of which have been a great help with assistance in translations and kanji information, let alone supporting individual learning. Mark Tankosich and Joe Swift have been especially helpful.

EJMAS

Another great source of information. www.ejmas.com

www.24fightingchickens.com

Rob Redmond's site provides much food for thought.

Classical Fighting Arts Magazine

Many of the articles have inspired parts of this book. www.dragon-tsunami.org/Cfa/Pages/cfahome.htm

www.russellstutely.com

Russell has been acknowledged as Europe's Leading Authority on the use of Acupressure Points in the Martial Arts. One of the leading sources of inspiration in street useable Kata Bunkai.

Over the last 8 years, Russell has been instrumental in dragging Traditional Martial Arts kicking and screaming into the 21st Century.

Never one to rest on his laurels he has continued to train and develop every aspect of Kata Bunkai, Self Defence and indeed the sporting applications of the Arts.

Russell is a regular Columnist for Britain's most prestigious Martial Arts magazines, Martial Arts Illustrated, Traditional Karate and Combat. He is in constant demand on the seminar circuit, teaching his proven methods of the correct use of Pressure Points in Kata Bunkai, The OCFM Syllabus and street applicable self defence.

Russell has been instrumental in the formulation of the OCFM Syllabus that has been ratified Worldwide. He is in constant demand on the Seminar Circuit and also for Private Classes and the ever more popular OCFM Courses.

"Russell is great to watch in action" Peter Consterdine ~ 7th Dan Karate

"Russell makes Pressure Points so easy to use. He has transformed my Martial Arts" ~ Bob Sykes 6th Dan Karate ~ Editor of Martial Arts Illustrated.

"Russell puts the reality back into Martial Arts" Rich Mooney 8th Degree Kung Fu

"Waveform strikes are amazingly powerful ~ I have never been hit so hard" Master Mark Adlington 4th Degree Tang Soo Do

"Real self defence, made real easy. Russell and the OCFM is where you should go if you want to learn what your Art really means" Malcolm Keith 3rd Dan Ju Jitsu

See the website for Special Offers

SEMINARS | COURSES | TRAINING CAMPS | DVD's | VIDEO's | PRIVATE CLASSES | GROUP CLASSES